MW00875206

Expecting Daily Pregnancy Devotion

Sarah Coleman

sarahcoleman.com.au

Copyright

Expecting Daily Pregnancy Devotion

Copyright © 2013 Sarah Coleman

First published in 2013 by Sarah Coleman

ISBN 978-0-9581546-2-8

All rights reserved. No part of this publication may be reproduced, stored in a retrieval system, or transmitted, in any form or by any means without prior written permission of the publisher.

Scripture quotations marked "NLT" are taken from the Holy Bible, New Living Translation, copyright © 1996, 2004, 2007. Used by permission of Tyndale House Publishers, Inc.,Carol Stream,, Illinois 60188. All rights reserved.

Scripture quotations marked "NIV" are taken from The Holy Bible, New International Version®, NIV® Copyright © 1973, 1978, 1984, 2011 by Biblica Inc™. Used by permission. All rights reserved worldwide.

Scripture quotations marked "AMP" are taken from the Amplified®

Bible, Copyright © 1954, 1958, 1962, 1964, 1965, 1987 by The Lockman Foundation.
Used by permission. (www.Lockman.org)

Scripture quotations marked "MSG" are taken from The Message. Copyright © 1993, 1994, 1995, 1996, 2000, 2001, 2002. Used with permission of NavPress Publishing Group.

Scripture quotations marked "NKJV" are taken from the New King James Version®. Copyright © 1982 by Thomas Nelson, Inc. Used by permission. All rights reserved.

Scripture quotations marked "KJV" are taken from the King James Version.

Cover Design by Sarah Coleman

Dedication

This devotion is for my amazing boys, Oscar and Hudson. I love you.

Introduction

When I fell pregnant, I went looking for a daily pregnancy devotion that would encourage me during this special time. I could not find one. So, I began piecing together thoughts and ideas, of how to write a devotion for pregnancy that would be positive and uplifting.

I pray that *Expecting Daily Pregnancy Devotion* is a blessing to you, as you carry your bundle of joy in the womb. Cherish this unique time in your life. It is time to celebrate and have that pregnant glow. Expecting a baby is wonderful.

As you read, you will notice a few things. I refer to your baby as "she." I understand that many will be expecting a boy, as I was. For the purpose of this devotion, constant gender kept things simple. Feel free to read "he" if you are having a boy.

On a few occasions I also refer to a parent as "she." This is for the same reason as above. If you are a father, please take no offence.

Expecting Daily Pregnancy Devotion is not full of my stories. My intention was never to bore you with what I experienced. I always wanted *Expecting Daily Pregnancy Devotion* to be about three people: you, God, and baby. My desire is that as you read each Scripture and corresponding thought, you will feel uplifted and energised.

As funny as it seems, pregnancy can cause people to be negative and cynical. There is enough of that in the world already. You won't find it in these pages. Instead, your eyes will be opened to how God feels about children, conception, love, peace, strength, grace, hope, and birth. The Bible has a lot to say about pregnancy, enough to fill nine months!

I am so excited for you as you embark on the pregnancy journey. Whether this is your first child, or your tenth, be blessed as you read *Expecting Daily Pregnancy Devotion.*

PS. I have some FREEBIES available in addition to *Expecting Daily Pregnancy Devotion* that will be a great companion. I have **two podcast recordings** of sermons preached with the release of *Expecting*, as well as a **printable of scriptures and confessions** I personally used during both my pregnancies. To access the freebies go to sarahcoleman.com.au/expecting-freebies/

Week 1: Day 1

Genesis 1:28 (CEV) *God gave them his blessing and said: Have a lot of children! Fill the earth with people and bring it under your control. Rule over the fish in the ocean, the birds in the sky, and every animal on the earth.*

The God of Heaven has pronounced a blessing over you - have a lot of children. If you wonder whether God's will is for you to have children, Genesis 1:28 should settle it. God's blessing is to have a family. It is His will.

After God created humankind He blessed them and said, "Have children." His mandate has not changed. He wants you to produce a lineage. Inability to conceive is not a sign that children are not part of God's plan for you. God's will for you is to have a child. Offspring are a blessing that He wants to bestow on you and your spouse.

Decide to settle this in your heart once and for all: God wants you to have a child. No ifs or buts. Begin the journey of faith to receive what He has promised.

The Almighty has spoken: Have a lot of children. It is your destiny. Believe it, and receive it.

Confession and prayer: God wants me to have a baby. How exciting!

Week 1: Day 2

Hebrews 11:11 (AMP) *Because of faith also Sarah herself received physical power to conceive a child, even when she was long past the age for it, because she considered [God] Who had given her the promise to be reliable and trustworthy and true to His word.*

Yours and your partner's physical power to conceive a child is not dependent on being young. Nor is it dependent on whether your ovaries are in good working order. It is not dependent on your diet or exercise regime. It is not dependent on your partner's sperm count, and it is not dependent on whether you have sex enough, or at the right time. Your physical power to conceive is dependent on faith in God.

Sarah received the power to conceive simply because she knew that when God made a promise, He was faithful to bring it to pass. As you will soon discover, there are a plethora of Scriptures related to conception, pregnancy, birth, and healthy children. God wants you to have children, and the promises of His Word are yours.

Believe in faith that, like Sarah, God has given you the physical power to conceive a child. He is reliable, trustworthy, and true to His word for you.

Confession and prayer: I believe God, and see faith manifested in the physical power to conceive a child. Thank You, Jesus.

Week 1: Day 3

Psalm 127:3 (MSG) *Don't you see that children are God's best gift? The fruit of the womb his generous legacy?*

Children are God's best gift. Having and raising children is the best gift (apart from salvation and the Holy Spirit) that God can give. And it is a gift that God wants to give to you.

Imagine the way you'll dote over your newborn baby. Father in Heaven dotes over you more than that. He has presents, gifts, and rewards He wants to shower upon you, for no other reason than you are His child, and His love for you is never ending.

God not only wants you to have children, but it is a gift that He can give you. A parent might want to give their child private school education, but if the finances are not available, it will not happen. Father in Heaven is not like that. He wants to, and can, give you children. All you have to do is believe, and receive.

The Bible says God will give good gifts to those who ask. So ask away, knowing you will receive the precious child you desire.

Confession and prayer: I know that children are the best gift, and I believe that it is a gift the Lord has given me. Hallelujah!

Week 1: Day 4

Matthew 7:7-8 (NLT) *Keep on asking, and you will receive what you ask for. Keep on seeking, and you will find. Keep on knocking, and the door will be opened to you. For everyone who asks, receives. Everyone who seeks, finds. And to everyone who knocks, the door will be opened.*

Prayer is defined as a solemn request for help, or expression of thanks addressed to God. Any believer in Jesus Christ will tell you that it is so much more than that. It is connecting with your Creator. It is a supernatural exchange, with the power to transform what is seen.

When you pray, God hears. He hears, and He answers. You can be confident in that. You are speaking to someone who is not just concerned, He also has the power to intervene, and make things better.

As you pray for the child that you will hold in your arms, know that God hears. You may be praying that you fall pregnant. You could be asking that you don't miscarry. Whatever it is, God hears, and God answers. You have what you are asking for. You are pregnant. You won't miscarry. You will hold a beautiful, perfect baby in your arms. Don't be discouraged. Be confident that you have what you ask the God of Heaven for. Everyone who asks, receives.

Confession and prayer: God, I'm asking that I fall pregnant. Thank You for hearing, and answering my prayer.

Week 1: Day 5

Genesis 25:21 (NLT) *Isaac pleaded with the Lord on behalf of his wife, because she was unable to have children. The Lord answered Isaac's prayer, and Rebekah became pregnant with twins.*

The decision to fall pregnant is one you have (hopefully) made as a couple. You have no doubt talked in excitement of what your life will be like with a new baby. You have possibly already made decisions about the type of birth you want, and perhaps even discussed baby names. But have you prayed together that you will conceive? I don't mean have you prayed separately in your private prayer closet. Have you prayed together?

There is incredible power in the prayer of agreement. The Bible tells us that when two people gather to pray, Jesus is there (Matthew 18:19-20). Don't do this alone. Pray with your husband that you will conceive.

At times, fathers can feel quite left out of the pregnancy process, after all, they aren't the one carrying the baby. However, there are some parts of pregnancy you can share. You can pray together that you will conceive, and pray for your unborn child. Your husband is likely longing to be more involved, but unsure how. Pray together, and allow him to lead the prayers for your child. Set up a lifelong habit of praying together for your children.

Confession and prayer: I believe that as I pray with my husband for a child, the Lord will hear and answer our prayer.

Week 1: Day 6

Romans 9:10 (MSG) *And that's not the only time. To Rebecca, also, a promise was made that took priority over genetics.*

Science is amazing. Through research and discovery, humans have the power to manipulate male and female reproductive systems, even genetics, to create life. God has been doing it from the beginning of time. He is the ultimate geneticist, and He can control, and manipulate your genetics without being invasive.

Rebecca gave birth to twins because God's promise of children took priority over genetic inability. The Word of God says that children are a gift, reward, and blessing. God wants you to have children, and His promises take priority over genetics.

If a genetic problem is hindering you from falling pregnant, God's promises take priority. God has a healthy and whole baby for you and your spouse. Whatever you have been told in relation to your family line, or genetic history may be true, but God's promises override it. Be full of faith, the promises of His Word have supremacy over any other.

Confession and prayer: I believe that what God did for Rebecca, He can do for me. I thank You that God's Word to me, takes priority over genetics.

Romans 4:18 (NLT) *Even when there was no reason for hope, Abraham kept hoping—believing that he would become the father of many nations. For God had said to him, "That's how many descendants you will have!"*

If you have been trying to conceive for some time, hope may be dwindling. Health professionals, and others, may be advising to give up hope. If that is you, hear what God is saying today, "Keep believing, have hope."

Think of an older couple you know, perhaps your parents. You would say there is no hope of them falling pregnant, right? That was Abraham and Sarah. Everyone said there was no hope they would fall pregnant. But Abraham kept hoping. Abraham kept hoping because he had a word from God.

You may have been told there is little hope you will fall pregnant. You may be thinking, "There is practically no hope of me falling pregnant." Don't give up. You have reason to hope, God has given you a Word, and that is enough.

Confession and prayer: I have not lost hope. I have reason to hope that God will do what He said.

Week 2: Day 1

Luke 1:49-50 (NLT) *For the Mighty One is holy, and he has done great things for me. He shows mercy from generation to generation to all who fear him.*

This passage is from the Magnificat, the song that Mary sang to Elizabeth after she became pregnant with the Son of God. Mary was overwhelmed with praise to the Lord in response to her pregnancy.

Falling pregnant is a wonderful time, especially when it is something you have desired. Conceiving a baby comes easily for some, and not so easily for others. While Mary's conception with Jesus Christ came about easily, I can't imagine it was the kind of conception she had in mind.

Conception and pregnancy can, at times, throw couples some curve balls. Whether you have the ideal conception, pregnancy, or birth, decide now that whatever happens, you will praise the Lord. Don't allow situations to get you down. Pregnant, not pregnant, morning sickness, bloating, swollen ankles, natural birth, caesarean section, healthy baby, a baby you need to fight for: praise the Lord, and rejoice in God your Saviour.

Confession and prayer: No matter what happens in this pregnancy, I choose to rejoice.

Week 2: Day 2

Deuteronomy 7:14 (NLT) *You will be blessed above all the nations of the earth. None of your men or women will be childless, and all your livestock will bear young.*

Deuteronomy 7:14 is a promise of God, with conditions. The promise of not being childless is conditional to obeying the laws and commandments of the Word. If you live a completely holy life, God promises you will not be childless.

Are you completely holy? Have you ever broken a command of God? We all have. However, if you believe that Jesus Christ died for your mistakes, you have been made holy and pure. So that means the promise of Deuteronomy 7:14 is for you. If you are a believer in Jesus and the finished work of the Cross, you will not be childless. You are blessed more than anyone else. Your life is fruitful. Your womb is fertile.

Doctors, well-meaning people, and genetics may say one thing, but God says another. You are blessed, and you will not be childless. Stand on this promise and see its fulfilment.

Confession and prayer: I am a believer in Jesus Christ, and declare the promise that I will have a child. I will not be childless.

Week 2: Day 3

Genesis 21:7 (First Edition, New Living Translation) *Who would have dreamed that I would ever have a baby?*

Today, it is time to dream. Dream that you perform a positive pregnancy test. Picture a healthy baby in the ultrasound. Imagine you have a pregnant belly. Envisage holding a perfect baby. See the dream of having a child fulfilled.

We read in the New Testament, that Abraham and Sarah are inspirational figures in our walk of faith. Things didn't work out for them first try. At times they were discouraged and made mistakes. But they kept the dream alive, and saw its fulfilment in Isaac.

Whether you are reading this devotional after trying unsuccessfully to have a baby for many years, or you are just starting out on the pregnancy journey, dream about your baby. Don't let disappointment, doubt, and devastation rob you of beautiful dreams. Nothing is achieved without dreaming it first. Set your heart to dream about your gorgeous baby.

Who would have dreamed that you would have a baby? You.

Confession and prayer: Father, I ask You to fill my thoughts with wonderful dreams of my baby. This is not false hope, because faith will bring this desire to pass.

Week 2: Day 4

1 Samuel 1:11 (MSG) *Then she made a vow: Oh, GOD-of-the-Angel-Armies, if you'll take a good, hard look at my pain, if you'll quit neglecting me and go into action for me by giving me a son, I'll give him completely, unreservedly to you. I'll set him apart for a life of holy discipline.*

Hannah is one of the most lovely characters in the Bible. When I read her story in 1 Samuel, I imagine a petite woman, with a kind, and humble nature. Strong, but at times fragile.

Probably the thing that strikes me most about Hannah's story is her motivation for having a child. Hannah did not want a son to keep her company in old age. She did not want a son because she felt that he would complete her life. Hannah wanted a son so that she could dedicate him to the Lord. Her ultimate motivation for having a baby was to raise a godly and upright child, who would live dedicated to God.

See yourself as the parent of a child who loves God, and has dedicated her life to serve Him. Determine that you and your partner will be people who set the best example for your children. It is not the responsibility of the crèche or Sunday School to show your child how to live for Christ. That is why God is giving this child to you – for you to raise in a godly way, dedicated to Him.

Confession and prayer: Father, Thank You for the privilege of being a parent. My desire is to raise a child who will love, and be devoted to You. Thank You for Your enabling power to do this.

Week 2: Day 5

Genesis 49:25-26a (NLT) *May the God of your father help you; May the Almighty bless you with the blessings of the Heavens above, and blessings of the watery depths below, and blessings of the breasts and womb. May the blessings of your father surpass the blessings of the ancient mountains, reaching to the heights of the eternal hills.*

The above verse is taken from the blessing pronounced over Joseph by his father, Israel. It is a blessing of overabundance. A blessing of insurmountable favour and reward.

Your womb is blessed. Not only is it blessed, but it is incredibly, superabundantly blessed. It is the perfect place for a baby to grow and develop. It will carry, nourish, and feed your baby with all the blessings of the Lord.

Over the next few days, as the beginnings of your baby travel down the fallopian tubes, and into the uterus where she will implant, confess that your womb is blessed. Confess that as baby, and the associated cells, arrive in your womb, they embed in your uterine wall without problem or obstruction, because your womb is blessed.

This blessing may have been pronounced over Joseph, but you can make it your own. Your womb is superabundantly blessed, and nothing will stop the blessing of the Lord flowing to you.

Confession and prayer: Thank You, Lord, for blessing my womb. You have made it a favourable place for my baby to attach herself, grow, and develop.

Genesis 4:1 (NLT) *Now Adam had sexual relations with his wife, Eve, and she became pregnant. When she gave birth to Cain, she said, "With the LORD's help, I have produced a man!"*

Cain means, "With the Lord's help I produced a man." The story of Cain does not finish well in the Bible, but it has a great start. His life started with the Lord's help. It is important to recognise that no matter how fertile, young, or robust you are, or how healthy your womb is, you cannot produce a baby without God. It all starts with Him.

It was a given that Eve would have children. She was incredibly fertile, and well able to birth many descendants, yet she acknowledged that God helped her. Eve recognised that the amazing gift of having a child came from Almighty God. She chose not to take pregnancy and birth for granted, instead she acknowledged God.

If the path towards falling pregnant, thus far, has been one of stress, worry, and turmoil, start acknowledging the Lord. Agree that He will help you fall pregnant, and that He will grow your baby for nine months in the womb. When you do that, not only does it relieve you and your partner of pressure, it also will make the path to falling pregnant one of peace and protection. What a wonderful way for a child to come into the world.

Confession and prayer: Today, I acknowledge that conceiving, and giving birth to a child will happen with the Lord's help.

Week 2: Day 7

Proverbs 30:15-16 (NLT) *There are three things that are never satisfied—no, four that never say, "Enough!":the grave, the barren womb, the thirsty desert, the blazing fire.*

You may have thought that it is not God's desire for you to have children, which is why you have been barren. It is not the case. The message of Proverbs 30 is don't be satisfied. The barren womb is not supposed to be satisfied until a child is growing there. Your womb is meant to be full, and only then should it be satisfied.

Your dissatisfaction in this area is not wrong. Now, I don't mean that dissatisfaction can turn to depression, disillusionment, or bitterness. God doesn't owe you. However, don't lose all hope either. Use your discontent to fuel hope and faith. Let dissatisfaction cause you to pray, and thank God for the child that will fill your womb.

It is not your time to say enough. Keep crying out for more. Our God is a God of more than enough. You will soon shout for joy because your womb will be full.

Confession and prayer: I am not giving up believing, praying, and thanking God that a baby will fill my womb. I will not allow the wait to wear me down so that I am satisfied with barrenness. I know, Lord, that the desire to have a child is from You, and I will not be satisfied until my womb is full.

Week 3: Day 1

Isaiah 54:1 (MSG) *"Sing, barren woman, who has never had a baby. Fill the air with song, you who've never experienced childbirth! You're ending up with far more children than all those childbearing women." GOD says so!*

Isn't it great to know what God says. The doctor might say, "You will never have any children." Your mind might say, "You're too old to have children," or "You have severe fertility problems, you'll never have children." Well meaning people might say, "God has blessed you with other wonderful things instead of children." But God says, "Sing because you're ending up with children."

That's why it's so good to know what God says. Other voices may leave you hopeless and in despair, but God's voice will bring success and rejoicing.

Notice that Isaiah commands the woman to sing before she has children. She is told to rejoice when she isn't even pregnant. You see, there is purpose behind the barren woman's rejoicing. He does not say to rejoice because God is good nor does He tell her to rejoice because of all the good things God has done for her in the past. No, Isaiah tells the woman, who has not had a child and is not yet pregnant, to sing because she will have children.

If your womb is barren right now Isaiah is speaking to you. His advice is to sing and rejoice, because you will have children. Other voices may advise differently but the best response is to listen to

God and sing. You're ending up with children, God says so. You have reason to sing.

Confession and prayer: Lord, I believe what You say. I rejoice in the fact that I will end up with children. Today I sing!

Week 3: Day 2

Ruth 4:13 (MSG) *Boaz married Ruth. She became his wife. Boaz slept with her. By GOD's gracious gift she conceived and had a son.*

The story of Ruth is one of the most lovely in the Bible. At the end of Ruth's life we find that she marries, and the dream of giving birth to a son is hers. Ruth's journey to this place was certainly not easy.

Ruth had her fair share of tragedy and loss, but her attitude is a great example of how to respond in such times.

In spite of her difficult circumstances Ruth decided that she would help others. She did not dwell on how badly done by she had been. Rather than be concerned with her own needs and satisfying her desires, Ruth showed kindness to others.

It is interesting that while Ruth was looking after others, God looked after her. It was while she was working to provide for Naomi's needs that Ruth met her future husband. God's gracious gift came to Ruth as she was gracious to others.

If the story of Ruth is anything to go by, and you want the gift of a child, be generous to others. God will look after your needs.

Life is not always fair, nor is it kind. Loss and trials come to us all. Ruth chose to be kind, and God looked after her.

Confession and prayer: Lord, despite what happens to me in my journey toward having a child, I choose to be thoughtful, and look after others.

Proverbs 3:5-6 (NLT) *Trust in the Lord with all your heart; do not depend on your own understanding. Seek his will in all you do, and he will show you which path to take.*

When trying to conceive it can be tempting to read, understand, and trust the report of health professionals, and others who have been in a similar situation. While there is nothing wrong with knowledge, it can often fill your mind with human reasoning and doubt. Instead, trust in the Lord, and He will show you which path to take.

God has everything under control. He knows when you're ovulating. He knows your body better than anyone. He also works miracles, and overrides the laws of nature in order that His will be done. He has enabled many women of the Bible to fall pregnant, and He can do it for you.

Stop relying on your own (and other's) understanding. Don't be anxious about what is going on in your body, second guessing every feeling and sign. Relax, trust the Lord. He knows when and how you will fall pregnant. He has a wonderful pregnancy path for you.

Confession and prayer: I trust in the Lord with all my heart, and falling pregnant is in His control.

Week 3: Day 4

Mark 11:23-24 (NIV) *Truly I tell you, if anyone says to this mountain, 'Go, throw yourself into the sea,' and does not doubt in their heart but believes that what they say will happen, it will be done for them. Therefore I tell you, whatever you ask for in prayer, believe that you have received it, and it will be yours.*

Jesus taught that you can speak to any mountain that you face, and it will disappear. Many people face mountains related to pregnancy, childbirth, and babies. Whether it is difficulty falling pregnant, the risk of miscarriage, or genetic disorders, you can speak to the mountain, and see it gone.

Even when you don't know whether you are pregnant, get yourself in the right frame of mind. Speak positivity and health over your body and baby. Believe you have received the glorious baby, pregnancy and birth that you are asking for.

Get rid of all doubt. God has the best for you, and that includes children. Refuse worry and anxiety, turn them into prayers and confessions. Problems and difficulties related to pregnancy are gone from your life. Nothing is too hard for God.

Keep this Scripture on your mind throughout pregnancy. Whenever you are tempted to worry, or if you get a concerning report, confess this immediately. The mountain is gone, and you have a perfect baby.

Confession and prayer: I speak to any mountain associated with baby, pregnancy, or birth, and I tell you to disappear. I believe I have received a wonderful, glorious and healthy baby, pregnancy, and birth.

Week 3: Day 5

James 1:17 (NLT) *Whatever is good and perfect comes down to us from God our Father, who created all the lights in the Heavens. He never changes or casts a shifting shadow.*

Every good and perfect gift comes from Him. Children are a gift. God gave children to families in the Bible. He was able to open the womb of women who were unable to conceive for many years. If God has given children to the women of the Bible, and to your friends, He will also do it for you because He does not change, and He is no respecter of persons.

God is not stopping you from falling pregnant. The devil is stopping you from conceiving, and he loves it when people think that his evil work is the work of God. Not being able to fall pregnant when you want to is not a good and perfect gift.

Believe that God will give you the gift of a child. Walk around saying, "I receive the good gift of a child from my Father in Heaven." You may think it's silly, but doubt is the devil's inspiration. Thoughts of doubt and fear will fuel the devil, and stop you from conceiving, but words of faith quench his fire.

Children are a gift from God. Believe it. Speak it. Have it. Take it.

Confession and prayer: God, I thank You that all good and perfect things come from You. I thank You for the good and perfect child You will give to me.

Week 3: Day 6

Genesis 18:13-14 (NLT) *Then the LORD said to Abraham, "Why did Sarah laugh? Why did she say, 'Can an old woman like me have a baby?' Is anything too hard for the LORD? I will return about this time next year, and Sarah will have a son."*

Is anything too hard for the Lord? Obviously Sarah thought so. She was nearly ninety years old. She had been married and making love to her husband for a long time. They may not have had ovulation calculators, but they didn't have contraception either. In around seventy years of love making, Abraham and Sarah had never produced offspring.

You may have been trying to conceive for a long time, not seventy years, but still a long time. It may seem like things are impossible for you and your partner. Don't give up. Is anything too hard for the Lord? Certainly not.

While it may seem rude, and even a little obnoxious, that Sarah laughed at God when He said that she would have a son, there is something we can learn from her attitude. Sarah laughed. Trying to conceive can be a stressful time for many couples. Ovulation applications and fertility clinics can turn the joy of sex into a time where husband and wife feel under a lot of pressure.

Sarah laughed. She may have doubted that she would conceive, but she didn't put herself or her husband under any pressure either. Sarah didn't let the thought of conceiving a child stress her out. She got on with her daily life and in time, she fell pregnant, as God had promised.

Confession and prayer: Father, I know that nothing is impossible to you. I laugh, because I know that my future involves a beautiful child. That is what I fix my thoughts on.

Week 3: Day 7

Genesis 30:22 (KJV) *And God remembered Rachel, and God hearkened to her, and opened her womb.*

Once your egg is fertilised, the new baby (scientifically called a blastocyte – not such a nice sounding name for a gorgeous new life), will travel down the fallopian tubes, and lodge itself into the wall of your uterus. From that time, the womb will begin to nourish and feed your baby until it is born, roughly nine months later.

This will happen in your body in the coming days, so you might like to meditate on Genesis 30:22, "God remembered Rachel... and opened her womb." Insert your name instead of Rachel. Confess that your womb is open and ready to receive your baby. Envisage the presence of God in your body, preparing the right environment for your precious child. Your open, warm, accepting womb is ready to nourish your baby. There are no problems with the blastocyte implanting in your uterus. Your womb is the perfect environment for your developing little one.

God has not forgotten you. He remembers you, knows your name, and even knows the intricate workings of your body. He has opened your womb for the beautiful new life that has been created.

Confession and prayer: Father, I feel so precious to know You remember me, and have opened my womb. It is the perfect home for my baby for nine months.

Week 4: Day 1

Psalm 45:16 (NLT) *Your sons will become kings like their father. You will make them rulers over many lands.*

Psalm 45 is a beautiful wedding psalm that speaks of the character and love of a bride and groom. The sons that are spoken of in verse 16 have not yet been born. The passage is encouraging the couple to have a vision for the children they will have. They are to see their children as kings and rulers.

You can do the same. Have a vision for the children you are yet to conceive. See them as successful and upstanding children, confident and favoured. They will achieve great things. See them receiving awards and accolades. See them as leaders who make good choices.

This verse is also prophetic - your sons. Read it: your sons (and daughters). You have children. It is not conditional or a maybe, but a given. You will have children, and they will be royalty and rulers.

This is God's vision for the children you will have. You will have godly, successful children. Get God's vision in your heart, and make it yours too.

Confession and prayer: Thank You, Jesus, for the godly and lovely children that I will have. I believe and pray God's vision of success and favour in their lives.

Week 4: Day 2

Romans 8:32 (NLT) *Since he did not spare even his own Son but gave him up for us all, won't he also give us everything else?*

The free gift of salvation and eternal life that we have in Jesus is so wonderful. All we did was believe in the Son and the power of the Cross to take away our sin, and we were rescued from death and hell. Salvation is the first, and most important gift, that Father God wants to give to us. However, God does not want to stop with salvation. He has so much more.

God loved the world so much that He gave His only Son. It pained Heaven when Jesus hung on the Cross, deserted and estranged from His Father. God gave His most precious gift when He allowed Jesus to be sacrificed in our place. Since He already gave the best He had, He will gladly give us everything else.

So what is included in everything else? Whatever you want, including children. God gave the world Jesus Christ, of course He wants to give you a baby. Meditate on the enormity of the gift of Jesus Christ, then boldly come before the throne and ask for a child. It is not too much or too hard for Him. If He willingly gave Jesus, He will give you a child.

Confession and prayer: Thank You, Father, that You sent Your Son to die for me, so that I can obtain Your blessings. Thank You for blessing me with a child.

Week 4: Day 3

Isaiah 44:2a (NIV) *This is what the Lord says— he who made you, who formed you in the womb.*

Now that your baby has moved from the fallopian tubes into the womb, many changes are taking place in your body. For one, you may get a positive result on a pregnancy test. You may also feel the additional hormones changing your mood, and other habits.

Most importantly, your baby is being formed. Cells are replicating and differentiating. Although the embryo is smaller than an apple seed, organs and body parts are appearing. A beautiful miracle is taking place inside you, right now. How precious!

The thought to meditate on is this: God is forming my baby. The hand of God is fashioning and creating a perfect and healthy child. Everything is happening as it should. The placenta is fabricating itself to feed the baby, and the blastocyte is growing flawlessly.

At times, miscarriage can occur in these early stages because the blastocyte, or the placenta did not take shape properly. The promise of Isaiah 44:2 is that God is forming your baby in the womb, and the Creator only makes perfection.

Confession and prayer: God, I see Your hands forming my baby inside my body. I know that You only create perfection, and I thank You for this beautiful child.

Week 4: Day 4

Jeremiah 1:5 (NLT) *I knew you before I formed you in your mother's womb. Before you were born I set you apart and appointed you as my prophet to the nations.*

The baby growing inside you is known. God knows the baby's gender, hair colour, personality, gifts, and abilities. God knew your child even before she was conceived. It will be several weeks before you get a glimpse of the little one, or hear her heartbeat, but God sees and knows her. How wonderful!

Not only is she known, but your baby has a destiny. God has set your child apart, and appointed her as a prophet. A prophet is someone who speaks God's Word and destiny into a situation. He has created your baby to be a giver of His life and promise. As tiny as baby is, she has a purpose.

Cherish these next few weeks as you find out that you are, in fact, pregnant. Ponder that God knows your child, and destined her to be yours. He placed her in your family. He knows the gift that she will be to you and the world. You may be filled with wonder as to what this baby will be like, but God knows, and in nine months, all will be revealed. Enjoy!

Confession and prayer: God, I am so glad You know my baby, and have a plan for her life, even now.

Week 4: Day 5

Deuteronomy 1:21 (NIV) *See, the Lord your God has given you the land. Go up and take possession of it as the Lord, the God of your ancestors, told you. Do not be afraid; do not be discouraged.*

See, the Lord your God has given you a baby. Possess it! Do not be discouraged. Do not be afraid.

This is God's Word for you today. Despite what your body is telling you, despite the report of the health professional: a baby is yours. God says so. Possess it.

See yourself pregnant. Banish negativity. Don't allow your mind to think on a bad outcome. When the children of Israel first faced the Promised Land they saw giants, and felt incapable of possessing it. Forty years later, the giants remained, but their attitude had changed. They believed God. They believed that with the Lord on their side they could defeat the giants. The children of Israel could have possessed the Promised Land forty years ago, but because they didn't believe God's Word, it didn't happen.

The Lord has given you a baby. The giants may remain, but when the Lord is on your side, you have victory. Change your attitude. You don't have forty years to wander in the wilderness. If God says He has given you a baby, He has. That's all there is to it.

Confession and prayer: God, I believe that You have given me a baby. I may be facing giants, but I know when I believe Your Word, the promise is mine.

Week 4: Day 6

Genesis 9:7 (CEV) *I want you and your descendants to have many children, so people will live everywhere on earth.*

God wants you to have children - many children. This was God's command to Noah, as he and his family exited the ark. You are one of Noah's descendants. That means that this command is for you: have many children.

This Scripture isn't for some and not others. That's not how God works. God's will is His Word. Other people may have said that God doesn't want you to have children, but they did not read that in the Bible. God wants married couples to have children, including you.

God doesn't give a command without also giving the ability to achieve it. Know that God has given you the ability to fall pregnant, and give birth to healthy children. It is His perfect will. And your body was created for that purpose. Falling pregnant, and having children, is the will of God for your life. So go ahead, populate the earth. Have lots of children!

Confession and prayer: No matter what I have been told or believed in the past, I know it is God's will for my life to have children. I believe and accept it in my life.

Week 4: Day 7

Genesis 26:12 (CEV) *Isaac planted grain and had a good harvest that same year. The LORD blessed him.*

Over the last twenty-seven days you have been planting seed. Seeds of faith, seeds of right believing, right thinking, and right speaking. The Bible says that Isaac harvested of the seed he planted in the same year. You may have been thinking things like, "God doesn't want me to be pregnant," or "I'll never have a baby," for a long time. The good news is, that because you've only recently started planting good seed, it doesn't mean you'll have to wait many years to see a harvest. You can expect to see a harvest of falling pregnant, and having a baby, in the not so distant future.

Keep planting good seed. When thoughts of worry or doubt enter your mind, cast them out. Allow Scripture to fill your subconscious instead. Meditate on the Word of God, and what God says about your baby, on a daily basis. Don't talk to people who will cause you to doubt. Stop reading books and Internet sites that instigate anxiety or negativity. Listen to testimonies of people who saw God give them a baby. You will see a harvest, and be a testimony of the goodness and faithfulness of God.

Confession and prayer: Lord, I thank You that I have been planting seeds of faith. I receive the harvest of a precious child.

Week 5: Day 1

Leviticus 25:19 (NIV) *Then the land will yield its fruit, and you will eat your fill and live there in safety.*

This is yet another promise from God's Word that you can claim during your pregnancy. It speaks of being fruitful, satisfied, and safe. Of course, you can claim this verse for your family throughout your life, but let's see how it applies to pregnancy.

Being fruitful is something you especially want while trying to fall pregnant. Believe that you are fruitful, and able to fall pregnant easily. Believe you are so fruitful, you won't miscarry. Believe that your pregnancy will continue through to term. There will be no complications with your pregnancy.

Satisfaction is another promise of God. You will be satisfied with life. By reading this devotional, you are indicating that you want to be satisfied with a child (or another child) as part of your family. God wants to satisfy your desires. Believe that you will fall pregnant, and be satisfied.

Finally, you will live in safety. There are many problems that can occur in your body, and in that of the baby, while pregnant. Complications are not safe for you or the baby. Leviticus promises invulnerability for your pregnancy. You will not experience obstacles, and your baby will be born safely.

Claim the entirety of this verse for yourself, your family, and baby during your pregnancy.

Confession and prayer: Lord, I claim that I am fruitful, satisfied, and safe. I will fall pregnant, and give birth to a baby without problems or complications.

Week 5: Day 2

Proverbs 10:22 (NLT) *The blessing of the Lord makes a person rich, and he adds no sorrow with it.*

God wants to bless you. Blessing is what He does. It's His speciality. And in case you were wondering, God's blessings are good things. They make you rich. Rich financially, emotionally, relationally, and physically. They even make you rich with children.

The second half of this Scripture is vital to your understanding with regards to pregnancy – He adds no sorrow with it. Children are a blessing. God adds no sorrow with the blessing of children. That means there is no miscarriage, no morning sickness, no gestational diabetes, no swelling, no disease, and no malformation.

God desires that your pregnancy be a rich and positive experience. Pray this over your body and baby. You will not miscarry. Your baby will carry to full term, and be perfect. The side effects of pregnancy will not bring sorrow, despite what has happened in past pregnancies, or family history. Receive the full blessing of the Lord that makes you rich, and brings no sorrow with it.

Confession and prayer: Lord, I do not accept any sorrow with this pregnancy. Instead, I believe for a rich and wonderful experience.

Week 5: Day 3

Exodus 1:21 (MSG) *And because the midwives honored God, God gave them families of their own.*

When you care about the things God cares about, He cares about you. The midwives of Exodus 1 were Egyptian women. They had been given instructions from the Pharaoh, to see that any baby boys born to the women of Israel were killed. By eliminating a generation of males, Pharaoh would render Israel helpless, and ultimately see their people vanish from the earth.

At its core, Pharaoh was showing injustice to children. The midwives did not agree with Pharaoh's maltreatment, and chose to let the children live. As a result, God gave them children of their own.

There are many injustices against children in our world today, from famine, to child-trafficking. God cares about each and every one. The Egyptian midwives honoured God by letting the baby boys live – one at a time.

Injustice can be overwhelming. The way to tackle it is one at a time.

Here is the challenge: why not stop injustice against children, one at a time. Sponsor a child, give to an organisation that helps needy children. Do it because it is important. Do it because God cares about the least of these. But also, do it as an act of faith, for the child you are believing God to give you.

Confession and prayer: Father, injustice against children sickens me. I am determined to eradicate offence, and let children live.

Week 5: Day 4

Hebrews 10:36 (NLT) *Patient endurance is what you need now, so that you will continue to do God's will. Then you will receive all that he has promised.*

Patience. What a lovely word for such a painful thing. The last thing you probably want to be reading right now is, "Be patient."

Are you wondering whether you are pregnant? You may have found out that you are pregnant, and are elated. Perhaps you discovered that you didn't conceive this month. Whatever your situation, be patient.

Patience does not go unrewarded. Hebrews 10 tells us that you will receive all that God has promised. Don't lose heart. Don't give up. Be patient. Keep doing God's will. Keep confessing victory and success. Keep believing His Word. Don't let doubt and unbelief get the better of you. Refuse worry and stress. Be patient, you will receive all that He has promised.

Just think, when you do have that beautiful child you so desire, all the patience you developed in waiting and believing God for her, will come in handy! All the parents said, "Amen."

Confession and prayer: Father, help me continue to be patient. Thank You for the reward that is coming to me sooner than I think.

Week 5: Day 5

Psalm 61:5 (CEV) *You heard my promises, and you have blessed me, just as you bless everyone who worships you.*

You and I were created to worship God. Worship isn't based on feelings or the right conditions. It can happen with music or without it. In the presence of others or while you are completely alone. There are times when it is easy to worship God, and there are other times when worship is painful; when everything flows, and when it's a struggle.

Worship is about who God is. So start expressing who God is to you: He is Healer, King of kings, Lord of all, Wonderful, Prince of Peace, Almighty, faithful, just, true, lover, beautiful Saviour, provider, protector, ever merciful, the Beginning and the End, Lamb of God, Lion of the Tribe of Judah.

Worshipping and focussing on who God is puts problems in perspective. Things that seemed so big, become small in light of a Mighty God. He is faithful. He has blessed you in the past, He is blessing you now, and He will bless you in the future. Worship Him.

Confession and prayer: Beautiful Jesus, I choose to worship, and focus my attention on You. You are great, majestic, and faithful to bless me.

Week 5: Day 6

Proverbs 13:9a (NLT) *The life of the godly is full of light and joy.*

I am sure most would concur that a new baby is light and joy. It is so wonderful to hold such purity and innocence. Babies cause the hardest hearts to melt, and put a smile on everyone's face. Babies are a delight to their parents, grandparents, family, and friends.

The promise of Proverbs 13 is that the life of the godly is full of light and joy. If you believe in the finished work of the Cross of Christ then you are godly, not because of anything that you have done, but because of everything Jesus did. That means this verse applies to you. Your life is full of joy and light. Specifically, your life is full of the joy and light that comes from a beautiful new baby.

See yourself holding your new bundle, fresh from the womb. Imagine the glee and elation of the moment. Envisage yourself introducing your new baby to others, and the gladness it brings to them. Your life is full of all the light and joy that a baby brings.

Confession and prayer: Thank You, Father, that my life is full of the light and joy of a wonderful new baby.

Week 5: Day 7

Genesis 15:1 (NIV) *After this, the word of the Lord came to Abram in a vision: "Do not be afraid, Abram. I am your shield, your very great reward."*

The covenant we have with the Lord through the Blood of Jesus is far greater than the covenant of Abraham. Even so, the Lord appeared to Abraham in a vision saying, "I am your very great reward."

What rewards have you wanted in the past? As a child you would have been happy with the reward of a lolly. Getting older, you perhaps were rewarded with money. You may be hoping for some kind of reward even now, through work, or even a competition you have entered.

Whatever the reward, it pales into insignificance when compared to God of the universe. Yes, He told Abraham, "I am your reward." His Word to you is the same (and backed by the blood of Jesus), "I am your reward."

You have already won the greatest prize. He is all you could ever want. He is all you will ever need. He is your reward, and in Him is the blessing you desire. Meditate on Father God, and allow Him to be your reward today. As you do, you will discover, as Abraham did, that the blessing you desire is found in Him.

Confession and prayer: Father, I meditate on You, my very great reward, today. Reveal Yourself to me in a new way, I pray.

Week 6: Day 1

2 Kings 4:14 (NLT) *Later Elisha asked Gehazi, "What can we do for her?" Gehazi replied, "She doesn't have a son."*

Elisha was a prophet of God. There was a woman in the town of Shunem that recognised the anointing on his life. She decided to provide for Elisha by feeding him, and even building a home for him whenever he came into her town. Because of her generosity, Elisha wanted to give her something in return. When Elisha asked what she needed she replied that she was well looked after. What she was not willing to admit, was the one thing she wanted, the one thing she could not have – a child.

Many people feel as this woman did – their life is complete, they lack nothing, except the joy of children. And many, like the woman of Shunem, will not admit their pain to anyone.

But the One who knows all, knew that in her heart of hearts, the woman of Shunem desired a child. Her desire had not gone unnoticed. Though she may have been able to fool some, she could not fool God. He knew the one thing she wanted more than anything else, was a child.

You may have tried to push the desire for children from your mind. You have perfected smiling as if nothing is wrong, when you hear someone else is pregnant, although the pain is intense. Your life is full and complete. You don't want to seem ungrateful, but…

God knows, God hears. He sees your silent tears. And He answers.

Confession and prayer: Father God, thank You for giving me my deepest desires.

Week 6: Day 2

2 Kings 4:16a (NLT) *"Next year at this time you will be holding a son in your arms!"*

Elisha calls for the woman to tell her the exciting news, "I know you said that you didn't want anything for your selfless generosity, but this time next year, you'll have a baby!" But instead of being elated, the woman of Shunem replies, "You mean and horrible man, how dare you get my hopes up." (Okay, so I added a few more words for effect.)

Perhaps you feel like the woman of Shunem. You have hoped, prayed, believed, confessed, and nothing happened. Things are about to change.

Elisha's statement was fact. It was as sure as the sun would rise, as certain as the seasons change. You will be. Not might be. Not could be. Will be. Those words changed the woman of Shunem's life. They will change yours.

Believe the prophet. Believe the Word of the Lord. You will have a child. The God of Heaven is not mean. He does not get our hopes up, and then dash them upon rocks. He gets our hope up, and brings miracles to pass. If we ask for bread He will not give us a stone. If we ask for a child, a child He will give.

Next year at this time you will be holding a child in your arms.

Confession and prayer: Father God, I believe Your Word as fact. I will be a mother. I will have a child.

Week 6: Day 3

2 Kings 4:16b (NLT) *"O man of God, don't deceive me and get my hopes up like that."*

It's time to get your hopes up. God is about to do something wonderful for you. Expect it. It's just around the corner. The greatest gift you will ever receive (aside from eternal life) is on its way. You are having a baby.

A baby that will bring such joy and laughter. A child who will impart delight through every stage of her life. One, full of innocence. So helpless, in need of love, protection, and security. A beautiful spirit who will surprise you no end.

This is a unique and wondrous time of your life. Enjoy it. Don't wish it away. Don't spend it in worry or doubt. Don't complain, or think of it as something to endure. It's time to have that pregnant glow. Let everyone know your excitement, and that you are full of faith. You, that's right, you, are having a baby. Hopes that are up are far better than hopes that are down. Get yours up.

Confession and prayer: My hope is up, and I expect good news any day now.

2 Kings 4:17 (NLT) *But sure enough, the woman soon became pregnant. And at that time the following year she had a son, just as Elisha had said.*

Sure enough. Sure enough, she became pregnant, and had a child. God's promises are sure enough. His Word is sure enough.

You can be sure enough on gravity. You can be sure enough that day will turn into night. You can be sure of the tide. You see none of these forces, yet you do not doubt their existence. You can be sure there will be stars in the sky tonight. You know that stars don't disappear and then reappear. They are always there, they can't always be detected. Yet, their existence is a sure thing.

Likewise, your pregnancy is a sure thing. It is sure enough. Not because someone says so, but because God Almighty does. He says so in His Word. It is sure enough.

The story of the woman of Shunem is a good news story. It is a testimony to the faithful, watchful eye of the Lord. God gave the woman of Shuman the child she so desperately wanted. It will be your good news story too.

Confession and prayer: God's promise of a child is sure enough.

Week 6: Day 5

2 Kings 4:34 (NLT) *Then he lay down on the child's body, placing his mouth on the child's mouth, his eyes on the child's eyes, and his hands on the child's hands. And as he stretched out on him, the child's body began to grow warm again!*

Okay, so the Shunamite woman's story is not such a good news one yet. She gives birth to the son she's always dreamed of having. Then one day, when he is older, he falls sick while working. They take him back to his mother and he dies. Distraught, the woman of Shunam calls for the prophet. He comes and raises the boy back to life. Good news after all.

Disease and death are not God's will for your child. He has a perfect and healthy baby for you. Don't settle for anything less. The woman of Shunam did not accept that God would give her a son, only to take him away. You should not either. Your child is healthy, growing normally, and full of life. Stretch your hands over your belly and pray that over her right now. See her perfect fingers, beautiful eyes, and delicate mouth. Your baby, as small as she is, has the life of God in her. Anything less is not God's best.

Confession and prayer: God, I thank You that my baby is strong, healthy, and full of life. She is growing normally, and receiving adequate nourishment from my body.

Week 6: Day 6

Psalm 113:9 (NLT) *He gives the childless woman a family, making her a happy mother. Praise the Lord!*

You may have discovered in the last few days that you are pregnant. Congratulations! Praise the Lord! I mean it, praise Him. He has done great things for you so give Him the adoration and worship He deserves.

Such happy times await. Those close to you will be delighted. Even those you hardly know will be excited. It is natural then, that your Heavenly Father wants to rejoice with you too. He is not remote or far off. He wants to be part of the celebration, as much as your closest friend.

Allow the time of pregnancy, and preparation for having a new child in the family, to take your relationship with God somewhere different. When you become a mother, you will have a new kind of relationship with your own mother. All of your relationships will change to a certain degree. Draw nearer to God during your pregnancy, and spend time praising Him for the baby you carry. He's given you a family, and much more besides.

Confession and prayer: Father, I want to involve You in my life and pregnancy. I praise You for the baby growing inside, and endeavour to keep praising and rejoicing in this blessing with You.

Week 6: Day 7

Romans 8:25 (NLT) *But if we look forward to something we don't yet have, we must wait patiently and confidently.*

Yesterday we talked about rejoicing in your pregnancy. That may not be your story. You may be unsure whether you are pregnant, or perhaps you did not conceive this month. Romans 8 reminds us to wait patiently and confidently.

A negative pregnancy test may have been devastating these past days. Hope and anticipation have been stirring in your heart. You were convinced that this was your time, only to realise it wasn't. What happens now?

You try again. You start again, and wait another month to see if you have been successful. But this time, you wait patiently and confidently. Patience is one thing, confident patience is another. You can wait for something under duress, in worry, and frustration. Or you can do as the Apostle Paul advises, and wait confidently, knowing that what you don't yet have, you will.

I do not wish to belittle your grief or pain that you have not conceived a child as yet. But be patient, and do it with confidence. Now was not your time. It is coming. Confident patience is what you need.

Confession and prayer: While I may be disappointed that I do not have a child growing inside my body right now, I wait patiently and confidently, knowing that my time is coming. Thank You, Jesus, for that peace.

Week 7: Day 1

Proverbs 15:13 (NLT) *A glad heart makes a happy face; a broken heart crushes the spirit.*

"Smile and the world smiles with you, cry and you cry alone," is what my mother used to tell me when I was a child and needlessly upset. I hated it. I didn't want to smile, and I didn't care that I was crying alone. What I wanted was some sympathy, which she was refusing to give. Oh, how it annoyed me.

The Bible puts it this way: a glad heart makes a happy face. Let your heart be glad today. If you are pregnant, and beginning to feel the effects of morning sickness, be glad. Feeling nauseated means the baby is growing. Though you may feel tired, put on a happy face, it is good medicine.

If you aren't pregnant, you may feel like crying alone. Reading something upbeat may not be what you want to hear. Allow yourself time to grieve, but do not let your spirit be broken. The medicine you need is a glad heart. Rejoice in what you have. Disappointment will crush and wear you down – if you don't have a glad heart. Choose to be happy despite your circumstances.

Confession and prayer: I choose to have a glad heart today. No matter what happens, I will never allow my spirit to be broken.

Week 7: Day 2

Genesis 33:11a (NLT) *"...God has been very gracious to me. I have more than enough."*

Jacob made this statement when he was reconciled to his estranged brother, Esau. It was a great blessing that Jacob's relationship with his brother was restored, especially after the deception that occurred. Even more wonderful was the fact that Jacob could say, "I have more than enough. God has been gracious to me."

Jacob was blessed financially, and with a large family. He experienced his share of trouble, conflict, and struggles, but at the end of the day, Jacob succeeded. Jacob understood that his success was not because he was a great business person, or someone of integrity. God was gracious to him. That is why he had more than enough.

Can you say the same? Has God shown you mercy? Has He been good to you? Are you contently blessed? I'm sure you are. When you recognise that you are blessed by His grace, you will find reconciliation, restoration, and greater blessings flow.

Confession and prayer: Father, thank You for Your grace. Thank You for Your abundance in my life.

Week 7: Day 3

Luke 1:42 (NLT) *Elizabeth gave a glad cry and exclaimed to Mary, "God has blessed you above all women, and your child is blessed.*

You are blessed and the child you are carrying is blessed. Your womb is a blessed place. Your baby is growing strong. The grace of the Lord is upon you. You are blessed among women.

Everywhere that you go, see yourself successful and prosperous. Feel the blessing of the Lord working deep within. You are blessed, not cursed. That means that anything associated with the curse is not yours, including pain, disease, or lack. Accept only blessing.

You may not be able to see your baby, or any evidence that you are pregnant, but she is blessed. Nothing will threaten her because of the blessing that is on you. As you progress through your pregnancy, continue to remember and meditate on the blessing of God in your life. Don't allow fear or worry to steal your confidence. You are blessed and your child is blessed. Blessed among women, what a privilege.

Confession and prayer: I am blessed, my womb is blessed, and my baby is blessed. Glory to God!

Week 7: Day 4

Psalm 17:14b (CEV) *You provide food for those you love. Their children have plenty, and their grandchildren will have more than enough.*

Right now, your baby might be small, but there is a lot of growing going on. And when there is lots of growing, there needs to be lots of food! God's got you covered. He supplies plenty of food to your baby. Your child has more than enough to grow healthy and strong inside your womb.

The placenta and umbilical cord are forming in the correct way. They will nourish and feed your baby without problem or obstruction. Your body is strong and healthy. You have all the resources, vitamins, and minerals to feed your child. Your baby is getting the right stuff to grow and develop. Everything is happening as it should in the early stages of pregnancy.

The Lord supplies, He is your Provider, and Provider to your baby. Throughout your pregnancy, your child has more than enough to thrive and live.

Confession and prayer: Lord, thank You that You are my Provider, and Provider for my child. Thank You for enabling me to have all the nutrition, and correct body mechanisms, to produce a thriving baby.

Week 7: Day 5

Deuteronomy 4:9 (NLT) *But watch out! Be careful never to forget what you yourself have seen. Do not let these memories escape from your mind as long as you live! And be sure to pass them on to your children and grandchildren.*

It is never too early to talk with your child about the good things the Lord has done. Even while baby is in the womb, talk to her about your faith in God. Tell your child that God has been good to you.

The benefits of reading to children is widely documented. Kids love a good tale. God repeatedly asked Israel to tell their children the things He had done. They were to be a story-telling people, except the stories they told weren't fairytales, they were real. When you talk to your children about the greatness of God, the blessings are two-fold. Firstly, they develop a love of reading and stories. Secondly, they learn that God is an awesome Lord, and nothing is impossible to Him.

It is funny that the world is only just recognising the value of reading and passing on stories. Talk to your child about the Bible. Tell them what God has done for you. Let your child's early memories involve chronicles of a wonderful family, and faithful God.

Confession and prayer: I will impart in my children the wonderful things of God. He has been so good to me.

Week 7: Day 6

Genesis 3:16a (NLT) *Then he said to the woman, "I will sharpen the pain of your pregnancy, and in pain you will give birth."*

You may be reading the above verse thinking, "Great, I've only just started. I'm suffering already, and there's more?"

Genesis 3 talks about the curse that was placed on woman due to sin. Because of sin, women can expect to experience pain in pregnancy and childbirth. That is the curse.

The good news is Jesus redeemed humankind from the curse (Galatians 3:13). Women have been redeemed from experiencing pain in pregnancy and childbirth. If you have been redeemed from sin, you have been redeemed from pain.

Here is what you need to do. Firstly, exercise your faith, and believe God that you will not experience pain in your pregnancy. Morning sickness is pain. Sometimes mild morning sickness can be a comfort because you know baby is growing, but when it becomes unbearable, and stops you from functioning normally, it is a curse. Christ has redeemed you from the curse of morning sickness.

Galatians 3:13 and Genesis 3:16a are partner Scriptures. Remind yourself of what they say throughout your pregnancy. When you feel any pain, or if something threatens your pregnancy, stand on Galatians 3, and the promise that you have been redeemed from pain in pregnancy. As you near your due date, stand on the promise that you will not experience pain in childbirth. The Bible says that you have been redeemed. The finished work of the Cross paid for you to be pain free.

Confession and prayer: Jesus, thank You for the finished work of the Cross. I believe that I will not experience pain in this pregnancy because I have been redeemed. I thank You that I will not experience pain in childbirth either.

Week 7: Day 7

Deuteronomy 31:6 (NLT) *So be strong and courageous! Do not be afraid and do not panic before them. For the Lord your God will personally go ahead of you. He will neither fail you nor abandon you.*

Not long ago I was watching a documentary of how babies form in the womb. At most stages of development, they explained in detail things that could go wrong during pregnancy. I was awed by the intricacies of creating a baby. However, in seeing the problems that can occur at every step, I was left feeling fearful.

Negative stories incite fear and worry. "What if something like that happens to me?" This is why the above Scripture is so important. God has personally gone ahead of you in this pregnancy. Do not be afraid or panic. He will not fail you.

If you are faced with a problem during pregnancy at any time, the first person to run to is God – not your doctor, or health professional, and certainly not the internet. The promise of Deuteronomy is that God has gone before you. He is creating the perfect child in your womb. Do not panic. Be strong, knowing that everything will be alright.

Confession and prayer: Father, thank You for going before me. I will not fear anything that may happen. I know that everything will work together for good.

Week 8: Day 1

Isaiah 44:22 (NLT) *Let all the world look to me for salvation! For I am God; there is no other.*

Isaiah makes it sound so simple: Look to God, there is no other. In Him you will find answers, and your needs will be met. Our enemy knows this as fact. His tactic is not to stop you from believing in the power of God, he wants to distract you. He sets up all kinds of diversions, so you won't look to God, and receive the salvation you need.

Distractions while you are pregnant take various forms: worry, threatening reports, feeling things in your body, not feeling things in your body, arguments, discussions, the internet, I could go on. My encouragement today is to get your eyes off the disturbance and on to Christ. Satan knows that you are a believer in Jesus, and the power of the Cross. He won't try to attack your belief system, but if he can distract you, it produces the same result. Be wise to his schemes and confusions. See them for what they are, lay them aside, and look to God for salvation.

Distractions are anything that causes worry, lack of sleep, confusion, or fear. Looking to God on the other hand will fill you with faith and peace for a delightful future. He is God like no other, look to Him.

Confession and prayer: God, I look to You today. Help me to recognise distractions. I will not let them take my focus from You, and the promises You have given me.

Week 8: Day 2

Hebrews 6:12 (NIV) *We do not want you to become lazy, but to imitate those who through faith and patience inherit what has been promised.*

The way that you will receive a healthy pregnancy, birth, baby, and anything for that matter, is through faith and patience. They are far more effective together than they are alone.

So how do faith and patience apply to pregnancy and babies? You cannot see what is going on inside your body. Early on, faith is what you rely on to know that you are, in fact, pregnant. You have faith every day that your baby is healthy, and developing perfectly.

You are pregnant for nine months. It will require patience to be joyful every day of your pregnancy, despite feeling squeamish, fat, or otherwise. After being patient for nine months you will then inherit what is promised.

Hebrews says we are to imitate other people who exercised faith and patience, such as Abraham, Sarah, Joseph, or Moses. Read their stories, and allow the Word of God to build greater faith and patience in you.

Confession and prayer: Father, I put faith and patience to work in my life. I receive the healthy pregnancy, birth, and baby that You have promised.

James 1:6 (NIV) *But when you ask, you must believe and not doubt, because the one who doubts is like a wave of the sea, blown and tossed by the wind.*

What are you asking for in your pregnancy, birth, and baby? Do you want a whole and healthy baby? Do you want reduced morning sickness? Do you want a pain free delivery? Have you been asking for these things? What are you waiting for? Go ahead, ask God. Be specific. Ask Him for exactly the kind of baby, pregnancy, and delivery you want.

That's the first step. The second is believe, and not doubt. Despite what others are telling you, and the horror stories you hear, believe God for what you are asking, and do not doubt.

There will be times in your pregnancy when doubts will try to crowd your mind. If you let them, you will feel like you are being tossed by the sea. Come back to this Scripture: believe and do not doubt. God desires to give you what you are asking for. Only believe.

Confession and prayer: Father, today I come to You, and ask for a healthy baby, pregnancy, and delivery. I believe and do not doubt that I receive these things.

Week 8: Day 4

Psalm 139:13 (NLT) *You made all the delicate, inner parts of my body and knit me together in my mother's womb.*

The God of Heaven is knitting together all the delicate parts of your baby's body, inside your womb. This miracle is going on in your body right now. How breathtaking!

By now your baby has a heartbeat, and her brain is becoming more complex. Baby has arms that bend at the elbows, and even a cute button nose (or at least the makings of one). Delicate hands, fingers, feet, and toes are beginning to form. Lungs and other internal organs are taking shape. Baby may still be an embryo, but she has all the makings of a little person.

Pray for your child as she is developing today. Imagine the beautiful work of art that is happening inside your womb. Look forward in anticipation, to the day when you will see this incredible masterpiece face to face. God is doing a wonderful thing inside you. Ponder that.

Confession and prayer: Father, I count it such a privilege to be a parent. Thank You for the miracle of life that is taking place in my womb. All the delicate, beautiful parts of my baby are being knit together. Amazing!

Week 8: Day 5

Exodus 1:16 (NLT) *"When you help the Hebrew women as they give birth, watch as they deliver. If the baby is a boy, kill him; if it is a girl, let her live."*

They say that two of every five pregnancies end in miscarriage. Have no doubt, the devil hates life. He wants to take your baby like he wanted to kill all the male babies at the time of Exodus. Don't stand for it.

We live in a time of such great technological advancement, yet when it comes to falling pregnant, there is only so much doctors can do. Miscarriage happens, and medicine can't give a reason.

The devil hates new life. He knows that each child has a divine destiny and plan. He can't afford to let any live. The next child born could be the catalyst for revival. She could be like Moses, and release people from slavery to things that hold them back.

It is so important that you begin a lifelong habit of praying for your child. The devil wants her life. Stand in the gap, and pray that she is protected, and safe from any plan or weapon he has set against her. Plead the blood of Jesus over her. The devil will try to destroy baby with all his might, but we have the name of Jesus, which defeats him and his schemes, every time.

Confession and prayer: Father, I pray for my baby. I cover her with the Blood of Jesus. I pray Your protection and safety over baby in my uterus, and for the rest of her life.

Week 8: Day 6

Malachi 3:11 (MKJV) *And I will rebuke your devourer, and he shall not decay the fruit of your ground against you; nor shall your vine miscarry against you in the field, says Jehovah of Hosts.*

This is one of the only places in the Bible that you will find the word "miscarry" (and this is one of the only translations that uses the word as well). The verse is specifically talking about grape vines not losing fruit before it is ripe. If grapes fall to the ground before harvesting, they are wasted, and the harvest is minimised.

This particular passage in Malachi is quite famous, because it speaks about the tithe. Tithing is a Biblical principle where you give God ten percent of your income, and live off the remainder. It is a principle that some unbelievers use, either saving ten percent, or giving to charity. Malachi 3:11 is included in the promises to those who tithe. It proclaims that if you tithe, your life will be fruitful, and you won't miscarry.

Miscarriage is devastating. It is not something that God desires for your life. If you tithe to the Lord, you can claim this promise. You can believe that your pregnancy will not end in miscarriage at any stage because God will rebuke the devourer on your behalf. The Lord wants to open the windows of Heaven and shower blessing upon you. You will not miscarry.

Confession and prayer: Father, I believe that I will not miscarry because You rebuke the devourer for my sake. I am abundantly blessed.

Week 8: Day 7

John 10:10 (NIV) *The thief comes only to steal and kill and destroy; I have come that they may have life, and have it to the full.*

Jesus came to give your baby life to the full. Satan may want to kill, steal, and destroy your child, but the power of life in Christ Jesus is stronger. Your baby is full of life.

Your baby has the life of God flowing through every cell. You have the life of God in your womb, providing nutrients, and nourishment to your child. Do not worry. You will not miscarry. Your baby has abundant life.

Declare this over your child each day. Jesus came to give baby abundant life. The Blood of Jesus protects her against any attack of the enemy that tries to steal, kill, or destroy her life and divine destiny. Jesus is the Good Shepherd who He watches over you and your child. Goodness and mercy are following you on the path of life. He is a comfort and shelter you can rely on. Life to the full is what you can expect for your child.

Confession and prayer: Jesus, I thank You that You came to give my baby life to the full. Thank You for protecting my child.

Week 9: Day 1

Ephesians 4:16 (NLT) *He makes the whole body fit together perfectly. As each part does its own special work, it helps the other parts grow, so that the whole body is healthy and growing and full of love.*

Today, Father God is perfectly fitting your baby's body together. Her whole body is healthy, growing, and full of love. There is nothing wrong with your child, and there is no reason for you to experience miscarriage. Your baby has a strong heartbeat and body. God is creating a faultless human being inside of you.

Your baby will run, play, and interact with other children. She will proudly show you the amazing things she can do. Your child will enjoy nursing from your breast and eating treats. What a day when you hear her say, "I love you," for the first time.

God is a wonderful creator, and He makes beautiful babies that bring joy and happiness. He is ensuring that all your baby's organs do what they have been created to do. He is allowing fingers and toes to grow, and everything to be in its place. Most importantly, He is placing His love in your baby so that when she arrives, she will be full of love for you, and all the special people in her life.

Confession and prayer: Thank You, Creator God, for creating this perfect person in my body. I know that You are making sure that her body is growing in the right way, and that she is full of love.

Week 9: Day 2

Isaiah 65:20 (CEV) *No child will die in infancy; everyone will live to a ripe old age. Anyone a hundred years old will be considered young, and to die younger than that will be considered a curse.*

Your baby is now officially called a foetus, which means, "little one." Yes, a little person is forming inside your womb. It is also a time when some people experience miscarriage, where their little one stops forming, and her heart stops beating.

If you have experienced miscarriage before you will know how tragic this experience is. You may even be feeling apprehension as to whether it is going to happen again.

Miscarriage is not God's will. He says in Isaiah that no child will die in infancy. No child. A foetus is an infant. Isaiah declares that she will not die. You will not experience miscarriage.

Claim this verse as your own. Your child will be born, and live to a ripe old age (but don't think of her growing up too soon, enjoy her being a baby). Your little one is protected, growing strong, and healthy.

Confession and prayer: Thank You Lord that my baby will not die. She will live and enjoy life to a ripe old age.

Week 9: Day 3

Psalm 36:7 (NLT) *How precious is your unfailing love, O God! All humanity finds shelter in the shadow of your wings.*

It is comforting and reassuring to know that you and your child are sheltered in God's love. His unfailing adoration for you and baby protects from any harm.

As baby is growing and developing, she is hidden in the shadow of His wings. That is such a precious thought. Rest in that promise today. Do not let doubt feed your mind. Allow yourself to be at peace, knowing your child is protected, loved, and held by Almighty God. Baby is hidden in a beautiful place of God's safety, where she can develop into the little person she is destined to be.

This child, who is so very precious to you, is even more beloved to Father God. Just as you unconsciously rub your stomach at different times through the day, God is cradling your baby. He will keep her safe, secure, and growing strong. Even the smallest of humanity finds shelter in the shadow of His wings.

Confession and prayer: Lord, thank You for holding my baby in the shadow of Your wings.

Week 9: Day 4

Hebrews 10:23 (NLT) *Let us hold tightly without wavering to the hope we affirm, for God can be trusted to keep his promise.*

Promises are broken all the time. Promises of love end in divorce, promises of loyalty end in betrayal. Even simple promises of being there, are easily forgotten. We live in a world where promises don't mean anything. They are often empty words. The trap we can fall into is thinking that God is the same. His Word is a bunch of empty promises too.

God is not like us. If He makes a promise, He keeps it. You can trust Him. Whatever promises God makes in His Word, He keeps. Guaranteed.

What promises are you holding onto in your pregnancy? Are you believing you will not miscarry according to Malachi 3? Are you holding on to the promise of pain free birth according to Galatians 3? Are you praying for a strong and healthy baby, full of life according to John 10? Know that you will receive these things because God keeps His promises.

Do not doubt. Do not waver. Hold tight to the promises you have. The Lord of Heaven will deliver.

Confession and prayer: God, I know You are a promise keeper. I hold tightly to the promises You have made to me, without wavering.

Week 9: Day 5

Ruth 3:11a (CEV) *Don't worry, I'll do what you have asked…*

While you are pregnant, many worries can fill your mind. From worries about your child's health, whether they will have any diseases or disabilities, to concerns regarding giving birth, and more. You don't have to be anxious for **anything**, God will do what you have asked.

You will probably find it reassuring each time you visit your medical professional, to hear your baby's heart beat, or see her moving and kicking inside your uterus. In between those visits, worries easily creep in, and cause undue distress. Don't allow this to happen. You have someone greater than a doctor to reassure you that everything will be okay.

Don't worry. Father God is looking after your child. Your baby will be perfect in every way. God will take your breath away with the beauty of your baby. He is a God who does what you ask. He will come through. He will not let you down.

Confession and prayer: Father, I choose not to worry. I know that You will do what I ask and pray for.

Week 9: Day 6

Genesis 18:12 (NLT) *So she laughed silently to herself and said, "How could a worn-out woman like me enjoy such pleasure, especially when my master—my husband—is also so old?"*

The story of Abraham and Sarah is fascinating. They were two normal people who had a visit from Almighty God, and their lives were never the same. From that time it was full of adventure, blessing, and believing for the impossible.

By now, you have possibly seen an ultrasound image of your child, and heard her heart beat. You are pregnant with a little person growing on the inside of you. Even still, doubts can fill your mind. Depending on things like your age and family history, you may be worried about your child. Now is not the time to worry, it is time to laugh. See a bright future for your little one. See her healthy and strong, and able to overcome anything that comes her way. Believe the best, not the worst outcome.

God works good in spite of our doubt. He knows how fragile we are, and how easily fear can grip us. Don't allow worry to steal the happiest time of your life. Be glad, laugh even. You are pregnant. Yes, you will enjoy such pleasure!

Confession and prayer: God, I won't allow doubt to steal this joyous time. I am thrilled that I have a healthy and strong baby growing in my womb.

Week 9: Day 7

Psalm 30:5b (NLT) *Weeping may last through the night, but joy comes with the morning.*

Miscarriage is something that happens to many couples. It is completely devastating to go from such joy of finding that you are pregnant, to hearing that the baby is gone.

Over the next few days we talk about the pain of miscarriage. If you are experiencing miscarriage, I pray that these readings assist in the healing process. For those who have previously experienced miscarriage, may these words continue the healing, and help you find new hope and joy in this child and pregnancy.

Understand this, God did not cause miscarriage to occur. We live in a fallen world where the devil steals, kills, and destroys - not God. God can certainly turn bad things into good, but He does not cause bad to happen. That is not who He is.

Satan caused the pain that you are feeling, but let your Heavenly Father bring you comfort. Weeping may last though the night. It may last several. But Father will help you to smile. You will be able to laugh again. Father God will turn this pain around, that is His specialty.

Confession and prayer: Father, I know you did not cause the pain I am going through now. Bring me comfort, I pray.

Week 10: Day 1

Lamentations 1:16 (NLT) *"For all these things I weep; tears flow down my cheeks. No one is here to comfort me; any who might encourage me are far away. My children have no future, for the enemy has conquered us."*

This can be how many feel when going through miscarriage. You cry more than you ever thought possible, you feel alone, and the child you once held so many hopes for, is gone. The enemy has conquered.

God understands your pain. It is okay to cry. It's okay to feel emotional. Miscarriage is a very painful experience physically. It takes a lot of energy and strength to deal with. On top of that, it is draining emotionally. People often don't know how to respond to miscarriage, which can be alienating, and cause more grief. Undoubtedly you will be comforted by someone you never expected, who experienced their own private pain. Miscarriage is not something people talk about because it is confronting.

When the grieving is over, rebound with a fighting spirit. The enemy may have conquered this time, but he will not conquer again. You will have victory in the end. A new day is dawning.

Confession and prayer: Father, thank You for letting me cry. In all this I know that I have won the victory. The enemy will not conquer again.

Week 10: Day 2

Revelation 5:5 (NLT) *But one of the twenty-four elders said to me, "Stop weeping! Look, the Lion of the tribe of Judah, the heir to David's throne, has won the victory. He is worthy to open the scroll and its seven seals."*

In the midst of your tears, the Lion of the tribe of Judah comes. In the tragedy of miscarriage, look, the Lion of the tribe of Judah has won. The Lion of the tribe of Judah is your rescuer. He brings hope, healing, salvation, life, and victory.

Look Heavenward today. See Jesus as He is - the strong, powerful, Lion of the tribe of Judah. He stands, in all His glory, at the right hand of the Father, interceding on your behalf. He prays for you. He is praying that the hurt will cease, and that you will join in His victory. He sees your weeping, and says, "Don't cry. I have won." Jesus knows what it like to experience pain, but He also knows this is not over. He has conquered, so have you.

Receive the rescuing hand of the mighty Lion of the tribe of Judah.

Confession and prayer: Lion of the tribe of Judah, I stop weeping, and receive the overpowering victory You have won.

Week 10: Day 3

Isaiah 53:4a (NLT) *Yet it was our weaknesses he carried; it was our sorrows that weighed him down.*

When you are going through miscarriage, the sadness is intense. You may be wondering if you will ever be able to smile again. But God does not leave us alone. He is our Wonderful Counsellor, and Comforter. He has the ability, to not just carry us through the pain, but exchange it for peace and hope.

After a miscarriage you can feel weak, drained, and sapped of life. Jesus carried your weakness on the cross. Exchange your weakness for His strength. Jesus bore your sorrows on the cross. Give them to Him. Give Him the pain of losing a baby. Give Him the hopes and dreams you felt for your child. Give Him your disappointment, defeat, and despair.

And in return, accept His joy. Accept His healing. Accept His hope and peace. Accept His love and comfort in place of all the emotions you are feeling. When you do, you will find it in your heart to sing again, because you will have children.

Confession and prayer: Jesus, thank You for carrying my sorrows on the Cross. I give them to you. I exchange the pain I feel at losing my child, and in return accept your peace, hope, and love.

Week 10: Day 4

Luke 8:50 (NKJV) *But when Jesus heard it, He answered him, saying, "Do not be afraid; only believe, and she will be made well."*

Luke 8 details the story of a man with a sick child. Jairus came to Jesus looking for a miracle. In the midst of his search, Jairus faced many disturbances - a woman looking for a miracle of her own, messengers telling him his daughter was dead, and mourners who had already given up. Jesus reassured Jairus, "Only believe."

During your pregnancy journey there will be many distractions and reasons to fear, worry, and give up on your miracle. You have one job - believe. That's it. Just believe. God will take care of the rest.

Good parents only ever want the best for their children, but there are some things that are completely out of our control. It is in those times when we must be like Jairus, and simply believe, leaving the rest to God. He is the Miracle Worker. Let Him fuss on the details. Only believe.

Confession and prayer: Jesus, I listen to Your voice today. I refuse to focus on the commotion. I choose to simply believe.

Week 10: Day 5

Proverbs 20:7 (NLT) *The godly walk with integrity; blessed are their children who follow them.*

We often see media personalities rave about the blessing given to them by a priest of a foreign god. Little do they know, that the greatest of all blessings is given to them by the God they learnt about in Sunday School, every time they sneeze. "God bless you." How easily we forget the immeasurable value in the Lord's blessing. He blesses the children of the godly.

Your child is blessed. God blesses your child as she is growing in your womb. Don't take this lightly. The blessing of the Lord brings wonderful benefits - healing, prosperity, success, peace, strength, to name a few. And unlike the blessing of the priest of a false god, the Lord's blessings produce tangible results. In other words, the blessing of the Lord works.

Be encouraged and excited that your child is blessed of the Lord. What God blesses, no man can curse. There is no greater blessing than His.

You have a blessed baby. Blessed.

Confession and prayer: Thank You, Lord, for blessing my baby. I treasure that blessing today.

Week 10: Day 6

Psalm 107:34 (NLT) *How he blesses them! They raise large families there, and their herds of livestock increase.*

Not only is your baby blessed, but you are blessed of the Lord as well. God loves to bless His people. He loves to bless families. His blessing brings favour and increase, both in your family and career.

See pregnancy as a time of blessing. Some people focus on the negative symptoms they are experiencing, and have an awful time. Choose a blessed pregnancy. See each day with your child inside your body as a gift. Once you give birth, you will never have your child this close, or this dependent on you again. Each moment of pregnancy is precious.

And don't forget to spread the joy. There is every likelihood that you will come across other pregnant women, and some of them will be negative and cynical. Bless them. Yes, bless them, their baby, and pregnancy. Let them know that they are blessed with the blessing of the Lord, the greatest blessing of all. For pregnancy is a blessing.

Confession and prayer: God, I receive Your blessing in my pregnancy. This is a blessed time for me. I am blessed.

Week 10: Day 7

Romans 4:19 (NLT) *And Abraham's faith did not weaken, even though, at about 100 years of age, he figured his body was as good as dead—and so was Sarah's womb.*

Sarah's womb may have been dead, but your womb is alive with a tiny person growing and flourishing. She is being nourished by your healthy placenta. Nutrients from your bloodstream flow seamlessly to your child as she develops. Baby is feeling the warmth, protection, and love of her mother.

Your womb is the perfect place for baby to grow. It is providing her with everything she needs to become a beautiful little person. New life is flowing through your veins.

Becoming a new mother can be daunting. Many think, "I'm not that maternal, how will I know what to do?" As your body automatically, and effortlessly knows how to create the right atmosphere for baby to grow, so too will you automatically, and effortlessly (okay, some parts of parenting come effortlessly and automatically, not all) know how to love, cherish, and parent your child.

Don't worry, you've still got a while to go yet! In the meantime, the life of God will flow through your womb, to your precious child.

Confession and prayer: Thank You, Jesus, for a womb that is alive, and a baby that is thriving.

Week 11: Day 1

Habakkuk 3:19 (NLT) *The Sovereign Lord is my strength! He makes me as surefooted as a deer, able to tread upon the heights.*

The first few weeks of pregnancy are especially exhausting. Feeling tired and nauseated may have been the sign that you needed to take a pregnancy test. Baby is so small, yet takes it out of you. Quite remarkable really!

By now, you have had enough of feeling this way. However, be encouraged. This is a sign that baby is thriving. You will soon be at the end of the first trimester, and most of your energy will return.

In all this, remember that the Lord is your strength. Habakkuk says that with God's strength, you are like a deer. So go on, feel like a deer, prancing through lush green meadows on a mountain. Okay, perhaps I'm taking things a little too far. But you can do all things through Christ. And if it is any less than prancing like a deer, I guess you'll have no trouble making it through today. God is your strength. This, too, shall pass in good time.

Confession and prayer: Lord, I rely on You to strengthen me today. Give me the strength to do all I need, and the wisdom to rest when I can.

Week 11: Day 2

Colossians 1:11 (NLT) *We also pray that you will be strengthened with all his glorious power so you will have all the endurance and patience you need. May you be filled with joy.*

This is such a wonderful prayer and thought that applies to us all, but it is certainly true for pregnancy. You need to be strengthened, not with usual strength, but with God's glorious power. You need His glorious power so you will have endurance and patience. Nine months is a long time. You've still got a long way to go. Receive the Lord's glorious power and be filled with joy.

God's glorious power and joy will cause you to do pregnancy well! You will have that pregnant glow everyone talks about, but few attain. You won't worry. You will not experience complications. You will not endure (or rather, cause others to endure) mood swings. Things will go smoothly, and everything will be a delight. When you feel yourself getting tired, irritable, fretful or otherwise, remember that you have the glorious power of The Lord on your side. You have what it takes to keep calm and carry on.

Confession and prayer: Father God, thank You for Your glorious power and joy, giving me the patience and endurance I need, to do pregnancy well.

Week 11: Day 3

Psalm 23:4 (NLT) *Even when I walk through the darkest valley, I will not be afraid, for you are close beside me. Your rod and your staff protect and comfort me.*

There may be times in your pregnancy when you experience a dark valley. Threatening miscarriage, premature delivery or a report suggesting illness or deformity in your child, are devastating circumstances to deal with. Whatever your dark valley may be, the Lord, your Shepherd, is there close beside you. Jesus Christ, the Good Shepherd, walks, and carries you through dark times.

Darkness does not last forever. You go through it. It is not your permanent state or condition. Don't be uneasy; Jesus is protecting you and baby.

He is the ultimate comforter. Allow Him to comfort you. He understands what you are going through like no one else. Give your concerns, pain, and confusion to Him.

It will be still waters and green pastures soon enough, until then, rely on the comfort, protection, mercy, favour, peace, and love of the Good Shepherd. He will lead you through.

Confession and prayer: Good Shepherd, walk with me through every dark valley I face. You are my comfort.

Week 11: Day 4

Psalm 147:13 (NIV) *He strengthens the bars of your gates and blesses your people within you.*

God blesses His people. Not only that, but He blesses the person within you. Isn't that nice? What a lovely thought.

Right now, you are one of the few people on earth who has a little person within. A little person who is blessed beyond measure, blessed as she grows within you. Feeling special? Feeling loved by Your Father? Are you feeling blessed?

Not only is the life within you blessed, but He strengthens you in the process. The blessing of the Lord upon your child, is a blessing on your womb and body, to prosper and thrive. Your baby is not a burden to your body, but a blessing. You are strong and healthy, giving life and nourishment to your child. Baby is blessed within you, from the nutrients given via your placenta. More than that, she is blessed from on high. Father blesses the one within you. The thought just makes you smile.

Confession and prayer: Father, thank You for blessing the child within me, and giving me renewed strength.

Week 11: Day 5

Psalm 92:14 (NLT) *Even in old age they will still produce fruit; they will remain vital and green.*

When it comes to pregnancy, there seems to be a magic number: thirty-five. If you fall pregnant beyond that age, things aren't so positive. You will be told that there is increased risk of deformities and complications. The good news is that the Bible says the opposite.

If you fall into the over thirty-five category, this verse is for you. Firstly, you will still fall pregnant as an older person, and you will produce healthy offspring. You will not miscarry or experience complications. You will have a vibrant child.

Secondly, you will remain vital and fresh. This means that despite being an older parent, you will be able to keep up with your children, and even grandchildren. You will be fit, healthy, and full off wisdom to direct and encourage your child in the way she should go.

Yes, you will have a child, and be a super parent, even in old age.

Confession and prayer: Jesus, I believe that I will have a healthy child, and that I will be full of youth and vigour as I raise her.

Week 11: Day 6

Deuteronomy 33:28 (NLT) *So Israel will live in safety, prosperous Jacob in security, in a land of grain and new wine, while the heavens drop down dew.*

Here, Deuteronomy speaks of abundance and security. These qualities are the desire of every parent for her family. Grain and new wine speak of prosperity. Good parents want their family to have abundance. No parent wants to live in poverty, or to have children going without. God promises to supply more than enough. He will send rain, causing everything in life to flourish.

It is important to feel safe. God promises security for families. A protected home in a good neighbourhood. A place where children are safe to play outside, enjoy the community, and go to sleep at night. An environment of love and acceptance, so children are free to themselves.

God desires that you and family are well looked after. It brings Him no glory when His people go without. His supply provides a good standard of living, being able to enjoy nice vacations, and make wonderful memories. His abundance incorporates healthy relationships and whole bodies.

God promises these needs will be met in Him. Our Heavenly Father takes care of families.

Confession and prayer: Father, thank You for showering my family with abundance and security.

Week 11: Day 7

Ezekiel 36:11 (NLT) *I will increase not only the people, but also your animals. O mountains of Israel, I will bring people to live on you once again. I will make you even more prosperous than you were before. Then you will know that I am the Lord.*

The best is yet to come. You may have lived an amazing life, and achieved great success, but the best is yet to come. God has more good things for you to enjoy, and children are just the beginning.

God will increase and stretch you. Children bring new and wonderful challenges and experiences. Your world will be extended in ways you never imagined. Children bring new dimensions of prosperity and joy.

When you have children, there are certainly things about your lifestyle that are sacrificed. Many couples sacrifice a higher income, and creature comforts when a baby comes along. However, God says that you will be more prosperous than before.

If you are looking at decreasing your income to have a family, claim this verse. God wants you to be more prosperous. He will give you ideas and inspiration to flourish. Don't settle for having to go without, receive the promises of God, and prosper even more with a family in tow!

Confession and prayer: I receive the promise of greater prosperity with children than without them.

Week 12: Day 1

Luke 2:40 (NLT) *There the child grew up healthy and strong. He was filled with wisdom, and God's favor was on him.*

Every good parent desires this kind of future for their child: a life of health, strength, wisdom, and favour. The Scripture is of course referring to the boy Jesus, but it is Father's desire that every child be the same. God's vision of your child's future is full of health, strength, wisdom, and favour.

You will have a healthy baby. She will be born a healthy weight, and will not need help to breathe. All her organs will function properly. Baby will grow into a robust infant and toddler. She will not be prone to, or suffer any illnesses.

You will have a strong baby. She will be happy and sleep well. She will have good motor skills, and develop good relationships with others.

You will have a wise baby. Your child will trust and obey her parents. She will honour authority, and be confident in who she is. She will make good choices all her days.

You will have a favoured baby. Everyone will love and cherish your child. She will receive preferential treatment. The hand of God will be on her. He will protect and provide for her, all her life. Your baby is a child of the Most High God.

Confession and prayer: Thank You, Lord, for my healthy, strong, wise, and favoured child.

Week 12: Day 2

Malachi 3:17 (CEV) *Then the Lord All-Powerful said: You people are precious to me, and when I come to bring justice, I will protect you, just as parents protect an obedient child.*

The Lord All-Powerful is your God. How wonderful to know that the greatest power in the universe is on your team. I mean, you can't get any more powerful than all-powerful. And He is using His power to protect, and watch over you and your baby.

You and baby are precious to God. He has His eyes on you. He is delicately knitting your child together in the womb. He looks on your exquisite little one, so fragile and small, with loving kindness. He gently cradles your baby and blesses her.

Injustice will not come near because the Lord All-Powerful is your protection. No sickness, calamity, danger, or disaster. Baby is perfectly formed. She is a picture of health.

No harm will come to you or your child. He covers your precious little one. He is using all His power to keep you and baby secure. You have nothing to fear. The Lord All-Powerful is watching over you and baby.

Confession and prayer: God All-Powerful, thank You for Your protection. I know we are precious to You, and are safe in Your hands.

Week 12: Day 3

Psalm 139:15 (NLT) *You watched me as I was being formed in utter seclusion,*
as I was woven together in the dark of the womb.

As adults we find comfort in Psalm 139, knowing that God watches over us, and that we can never escape His love. However, this passage has even greater significance when you carry a child in your own womb. There is a peace and reassurance that comes as you read the words of Psalm 139 regarding your baby. The Creator of Heaven and earth is watching your child. How special!

God is the ultimate project manager, in complete control of the most important venture He has ever undertaken - your child. No detail is too small, no task too menial for His undivided attention. He may have done this billions of times, but each one is precious. He gets a thrill out of designing and creating life, each and every time.

As your child lies in utter seclusion, complete darkness, Father watches. He lovingly ensures your baby is alright. He has a wonderful destiny in store. This is just the beginning.

Confession and prayer: Thank You, Creator God, for forming my child in utter seclusion. You lovingly watch over my baby.

Week 12: Day 4

Psalm 139:16 (NLT) *You saw me before I was born. Every day of my life was recorded in your book. Every moment was laid out before a single day had passed.*

Life is precious. No child is conceived as an accident. Every baby has purpose and destiny pronounced over her by the God of Heaven. From the hairs on her head, personality, and individual quirks, to university graduations and weddings, God sees and knows. Every moment. Every smile. Every tear. All laid out.

Father knows your adorable baby. He knows her personality. He knows what she will like, and what will make her cry. He knows the way her smile will melt your heart. He knows when she will crawl, when she will get her first tooth, and when she will say, "Mum" and "Dad." Father knows every loving moment you will spend with your child. He cherishes it, as you do.

Speak to your baby today, telling her about her wonderful Creator. Explain that she has a destiny. Express your excitement in being her parent, and that you will have many wonderful moments together.

God has a magnificent destiny and plan for you, baby. It is going to be incredible!

Confession and prayer: Father God, I am so excited by the destiny You have for my baby. I am looking forward to every moment I share with her.

Week 12: Day 5

Psalm 139:17 (NLT) *How precious are your thoughts about me, O God. They cannot be numbered!*

Even before you conceived your child, you may have had many precious thoughts about her. You may have imagined her nursery, or purchased clothes that she will wear. With that in mind, it goes without saying that God has had many more divine thoughts about your baby. So many precious thoughts, you cannot number them. Exquisite, beautiful, love-filled thoughts of her Father in Heaven.

God's thoughts about your child are good. He thinks about the good things that will happen in her life. The future He has mapped out is perfect. It does not include sadness, sickness, or trouble. Father imagines her prosperity and success. He is thinking about how much He loves and cares for your child. How He wants to bless this valuable life He created. Her beautiful future is on His mind.

Each time that you think of your baby, know that God has been thinking of her too. The precious thoughts that you have, were no doubt thought of in Heaven first.

Confession and prayer: Jesus, You think such wonderful thoughts about my child. Let me catch a glimpse of Your thoughts of her today.

Isaiah 44:24 (NIV) *"This is what the Lord says—your Redeemer, who formed you in the womb: I am the Lord, the Maker of all things, who stretches out the Heavens, who spreads out the earth by myself."*

Take a deep breath. Look around you. The world is an amazing place. Think about the night sky, the vastness, the stars, and planets. The universe is stunning. What a great Creator we have.

And that Creator, who stretches stars on His canvas, sculpts the child you are carrying in your womb. Right now she has legs that kick, hands curled up close, and a gentle face. Her features are becoming more recognisable as human, but her humanity has been real since the moment of conception. She is one of a kind, and blessed with the love of Heaven.

Nothing is too hard for God. He created a perfect universe for us to enjoy, and He creates whole and healthy babies to explore it. Rest easy in the Lord. He has everything under control. The God of the universe cares about the tiny child in your womb.

Confession and prayer: God of the universe, create a beautiful, perfect child inside me.

Week 12: Day 7

Luke 2:19 *But Mary kept all these things in her heart and thought about them often.*

Pregnancy is a special time in your life. You will only choose to experience pregnancy for a certain number of times, and then it's over. You will never be pregnant again, and there will be new parenting experiences and stages.

How you view your pregnancy and birthing experience is a choice. It is highly likely that things won't always go according to plan. You can complain about everything, or you can enjoy this time.

Mary would have encountered opposition and negativity regarding her pregnancy, considering her unusual circumstances. That was not what she remembered. She chose to recall the sacred and joyful moments.

Choose to have a pleasurable pregnancy, and remember the good things. Your child will want to hear about your experience with her in the womb. She will want to know how special it was to have her so close, not how sick you were, or what a struggle everything was. Cherish this time, treasure the coming months in your heart, and think of them often. It is a once in a lifetime experience, enjoy it while you can.

Confession and prayer: No matter what happens in this pregnancy, I choose to rejoice.

Week 13: Day 1

Psalm 46:1 (NLT) *God is our refuge and strength, always ready to help in times of trouble.*

Pregnancy affects different people in different ways, and no two pregnancies are the same. By now you are probably coping better, and feeling stronger because the effects of morning sickness have dissipated. But pregnancy may be affecting you emotionally, or even spiritually. In whatever you are going through, God is your refuge and strength. Run to Him. He is ready to help.

When things begin to overwhelm you, rather than have a meltdown, draw on God's strength. Nothing is too small for His notice. If it matters to you, it certainly matters to Him. The Lord is your refuge. Needing and relying on Him is not a bad thing. In fact, it is how we are supposed to exist - in constant reliance and dependence on His love and grace.

Let The Lord be your refuge and strength today. Whether you are struggling during pregnancy or not, He is there, ready help. The way He does best.

Confession and prayer: Lord, You are my refuge. I run to You for help in my everyday life, and this pregnancy.

Week 13: Day 2

Psalm 23:1-3 (NLT) *The Lord is my shepherd; I have all that I need. He lets me rest in green meadows; he leads me beside peaceful streams. He renews my strength. He guides me along right paths, bringing honor to his name.*

Life is good when the Lord is your shepherd. He provides for your every need; gives your heart rest; leads you; renews you; and guides you on the right path. Such a gentle and faithful Shepherd we have.

The Lord has provided all you need to have a wonderful pregnancy. You can rest and be sure that He is looking after baby. Everything will work out, despite what others may say.

Your baby is listening to the peaceful rhythm of your heart beat as she rests in your womb (a comforting sound that you may need to mimic when trying to settle her and put her to sleep). So too, the Good Shepherd is leading you by peaceful streams. Allow yourself to be renewed in His presence. If the last few weeks have taken a little out of you, stop and recharge with Jesus today. Allow Him to refresh and renew your spirit.

It is the Lord's perfect timing that you are pregnant now. It is the right path for you to take. You are not too old, or too young. This is the path He is guiding you through, He will bring honour to His name.

Hold on to these promises from the Good Shepherd today.

Confession and prayer: Lord, You are my shepherd. Renew me, guide me, and give me rest in Your presence.

Week 13: Day 3

Jeremiah 17:5-6 (NKJV) *Cursed is the man who trusts in man and makes flesh his strength, whose heart departs from the Lord. For he shall be like a shrub in the desert, and shall not see when good comes, but shall inhabit the parched places in the wilderness, in a salt land which is not inhabited.*

God has given you promises that you will have a healthy and perfect child. However, health professionals may be telling you otherwise. People may be advising you to terminate your pregnancy because of the problems you are experiencing. Who will you trust? Man or God?

Doctors and health professionals are necessary. Their words are based on experience and science. Their advice is trustworthy. But trust in man should not be put before trust in God.

Trusting in the opinions and advice of man, more than the promises of God has consequences. Jeremiah says one consequence is that you can't see when good comes. You are pregnant! There is a baby growing inside you. Have you felt joy and excitement by that lately? Or have reports, and possible diagnoses, robbed that from you? Stop putting all your trust in man, and turn to God and His promises.

When you put trust in man before trust in God, you find yourself in a wilderness of confusion and doubt. Heed good advice, but make sure that you trust God first. When you do, you will see when good comes.

Confession and prayer: Lord, today I choose to trust in You. I recognise the good you have brought across my path.

Week 13: Day 4

Jeremiah 17:7-8 (NKJV) *Blessed is the man who trusts in the Lord, and whose hope is the Lord. For he shall be like a tree planted by the waters, which spreads out its roots by the river, and will not fear when heat comes; but its leaf will be green, and will not be anxious in the year of drought, nor will cease from yielding fruit.*

Today we see the benefits of trusting in the Lord. The first benefit is a life of blessings, not curses. The second is a life that is stable and secure. The third is that when the pressure is on, you won't fear. And lastly, when times are lean, you won't be worried, instead, you will keep being successful and fruitful.

Let's apply that to pregnancy. When you trust the promises of the Word more than the words of man you will be blessed. The blessing will manifest in security and safety. You will feel confident and assured. You won't feel doubtful or confused. If you hear a negative report, your first instinct will be faith, not fear. And despite what is happening to others, your body will be fruitful.

Put your faith in Him. When you trust the Lord, you see the good in life, possess quiet confidence, and continue to be fruitful. Keep trusting. Don't give up now.

Confession and prayer: Lord, I put my trust in you. Thank You for making me confident, and fruitful in this pregnancy.

Week 13: Day 5

Mark 5:34 (NLT) *And he said to her, "Daughter, your faith has made you well. Go in peace. Your suffering is over."*

The past few weeks may have made you feel like you were suffering. Morning sickness, which for many women should be more aptly named all-day-and-night sickness, is a discomfort you may have endured recently. The good news is that for most, that suffering is over, and the majority of your strength and energy has returned.

This is an important milestone in the pregnancy journey - the completion of your first trimester. You are roughly one third through your pregnancy, and if this is not your first child, you probably can't hide the fact that you are pregnant much longer.

Second trimester is known as the easiest of the three. Enjoy the next thirteen weeks. Take time to spend with your husband, children, and yourself. Enjoy feeling good, and knowing that a beautiful baby is growing inside. The suffering of morning sickness is over. Go in peace.

Confession and prayer: Lord, thank You for the child growing inside me, and thank You for taking away the hardship of morning sickness. I will enjoy the second trimester.

Week 13: Day 6

Genesis 30:13 (NLT) *And Leah named him Asher, for she said, "What joy is mine! Now the other women will celebrate with me."*

If you chose to wait until the thirteenth week mark to announce your pregnancy, you are probably experiencing the joy, and celebration of others as they hear the happy baby news. Having a child is a wonderful thing.

Sometimes the news of a new baby does not bring joy. Maybe the pregnancy was unplanned and a surprise. Perhaps you're trying to be glad, but deep down, you're worried about paying the bills, and the expense of another little one. You may be apprehensive because of the problems you had giving birth in the past. Whatever it is, you're not delighted.

Leah is an interesting character from the Bible. She didn't have a happy marriage, she never felt good enough, and she was lonely and unloved. Leah had her own set of problems and issues to deal with. Despite that, she loved her children, and chose to be joyful and excited by them.

There may be many things going on in your life right now, but choose to be thrilled by the child you carry. Allow the enthusiasm and passion of others to rub off on you. Being excited betrays no one, but it breathes love and acceptance into your womb, and the heart of your child.

Confession and prayer: Lord, I am joyful and excited by my baby. I celebrate with those around me as I announce her impending birth.

Week 13: Day 7

Exodus 23:26 (NLT) *There will be no miscarriages or infertility in your land, and I will give you long, full lives.*

You have reached the end of the first trimester. Baby is alive and well. You have probably seen her heartbeat, and maybe even some kicks and squirms as you were prodded by the ultrasound probe. There is a strong and healthy little one growing inside.

God hates death and miscarriage. He hates infertility. It is not part of His plan. Long life is His plan. Lives full of adventure and goodness are His plan. That is what He promises to those who love Him.

Now that the danger phase of miscarriage has passed, begin to pray for a long, full life for your child. That is God's design. That is His will. In fact, He has a long, and full life planned for everyone in your family. God intends for you to be around for many years to enjoy your child. She will give you much pleasure and satisfaction. This is your heritage, and right as a child of God.

Confession and prayer: God, thank You for protecting my child from miscarriage. I believe that she will have a long and full life.

Week 14: Day 1

Isaiah 54:13 (NLT) *I will teach all your children, and they will enjoy great peace.*

The human mind is an incredible thing. As baby grows in the womb, she is learning. Learning the sound of your voice, the rhythms of your heart. When she enters the world the learning curve increases dramatically. Everything she hears, sees, tastes, smells, and touches becomes her teacher.

The greatest teacher your child has is the Lord. His wisdom and understanding far surpass any other. He has the insight to teach your child the way she will learn best, because He created her that way. He will teach her in kindness, and she will, in turn, be kind and polite. When the Lord is your child's instructor, she will have peace. School will not stress her or be a burden. Learning will be joyful and exciting.

Children are born with a desire to gain knowledge. The world squashes that hunger replacing it with rebellion. But when the Lord is her teacher, your child will love to learn, and have great peace.

Confession and prayer: Thank You, Jesus for being my child's teacher. Teach her to be like You.

Week 14: Day 2

Isaiah 49:1 (NLT) *Listen to me, all you in distant lands! Pay attention, you who are far away! The Lord called me before my birth; from within the womb he called me by name.*

Choosing a name for your child is a monumental decision, and one that you are no doubt putting a lot of thought into. Perhaps you have had your heart set on a name for a long time, or you are musing over a few at the moment. It is incredible, but God knows the name of your child today. He calls her by name as He watches and nurtures her tiny body.

People choose names for their children for a variety of reasons: the name of a relative, the name of a celebrity, how the name sounds, or they just plain like it. From the instant your child was first created, God knew her name. He knows your baby's name, and He has a plan and purpose or her. God has a unique calling on her life. Baby has been created with a specific mandate only she can fulfil.

Whatever name you decide on, know that it is the perfect name, and Father God is using it already.

Confession and prayer: Thank You, Father that You love my baby, and know her name.

Numbers 6:24-25 (NLT) *May the Lord bless you and protect you. May the Lord smile on you and be gracious to you.*

You are living in a time of the Lord's grace. Because of the complete and finished work of the Cross of Jesus Christ, your life is blessed, protected, and favoured. God's desire is that you prosper and succeed in everything you do.

God is not angry or upset with you. He doesn't shake His head or cluck His tongue in disappointment when you make a mistake. Instead, He smiles at you. That's right, He is smiling at you all day long. He smiles because He sees you as righteous. Not because of anything you have done, but because of Jesus, and what He accomplished on the Cross.

Feel the smile of Almighty God on you today. Your pregnancy is not a mistake. It is part of the grace and blessing of the Lord for your life. God is pleased that you are pregnant, and have a wonderful, healthy child growing inside.

Confession and prayer: Father, I feel Your smile and approval of my life. Thank You for making me the righteousness of God in Christ Jesus.

Week 14: Day 4

Ezekiel 37:7 (NLT) *So I spoke this message, just as he told me. Suddenly as I spoke, there was a rattling noise all across the valley. The bones of each body came together and attached themselves as complete skeletons.*

Ezekiel was a prophet. He spoke God's Word to a valley of dry bones, and they came to life - a mighty army. Like Ezekiel, you can speak life into situations and see miracles happen. You can see impossible circumstances come together, and be greater and better than before.

Speak to your baby. Command her bones to form and come together. See her flesh and organs forming also, just as they should. Your body, and baby's body, must conform to the Word of God. Baby's body is attaching itself in perfect form. She has a complete skeleton, and a complete body.

Ezekiel was faced with an impossible situation yet, as he spoke, God was able to breathe life into bones and lives. There is incredible power in our words. The Word creates. Speak God's Word. Speak life, and watch your baby grow into a mighty warrior.

Confession and prayer: Father, I speak life into my baby's body, and I see her become a mighty person.

Week 14: Day 5

Psalm 27:10 (NLT) *Even if my father and mother abandon me, the Lord will hold me close.*

We live in a world where there is easy access to information. It enables us to learn new things and stay informed, but it can also fill us with unnecessary fear.

Like every parent, you are doing your finest to look after baby the best way that you can. There are plenty of guidelines about what to eat, what not to eat; what to do, and what not to do, when you are pregnant. But sometimes, unintentionally, you may have eaten something you shouldn't have, or done something that you have since found out, could potentially harm your child.

This situation is nowhere close to a mother or father abandoning their child, but know that if you have eaten something that you shouldn't have, God holds your baby close. Don't fear. He is protecting her, and keeping her safe. Don't feel guilty or overcome with worry. Your child is in the arms of God, there is no need to panic. If you live a healthy lifestyle, and make responsible choices, be assured that God will do the rest. Baby is close to Him.

Confession and prayer: God, I believe You hold my baby close, and protect her from harm. I lead a healthy lifestyle, and don't worry.

Week 14: Day 6

Psalm 56:11 (NKJV) *In God I have put my trust; I will not be afraid. What can man do to me?*

It is wonderful to have a great support network around when you are expecting a newborn. Doctors, midwives, family, and friends, all make things easier in adjusting to the responsibilities of a baby.

For whatever reason, sometimes people who should be supportive, are negative and discouraging. It is hard to understand why people can be so hurtful.

Father God is your ultimate supporter. He believes in you, and He believes in your child. He promises healthy and robust children that live a long life. He promises a safe and comfortable pregnancy for you. Trust Him and His Word. Do not let the words of others cause fear and doubt. And don't take them to heart. Forgive those who may have hurt you. Refuse to dwell on their lack of support or negative comments. Mere mortals cannot do anything to you. Trust in the Lord, He will never let you down.

Confession and prayer: Father, I trust You more than I trust the words of others. You are a great support and refuge.

Week 14: Day 7

John 1:3 (NLT) *God created everything through him, and nothing was created except through him.*

Jesus is the light of the world. God created everything through Jesus, and that includes your child. The stars, land, trees, flowers, animals, and your baby, were made through Christ. He was there at the moment of conception, placing light, life, and love in her. This is such a beautiful and precious thought.

When you meet your child for the first time you will fall in love. She will melt your heart. The innocence and beauty of her soul will overwhelm you. The light that she shines is the light of Jesus. She is Heaven's perfection, created through the Prince of Heaven, Jesus Christ, Himself.

Your baby is loved, and adored by her Saviour and Creator. She is no accident. Her life has been predestined. Her body is beautiful, but more importantly, her spirit has been marked by the love, light, and life of Jesus. Baby is created through Him for His glory.

Confession and prayer: Jesus, thank You for shining your love, light, and life into my baby.

Week 15: Day 1

Job 31:15 (CEV) *After all, God is the one who gave life to each of us before we were born.*

Despite the circumstances surrounding you and your baby, God has given her life. She is His child and He loves her.

Perhaps this pregnancy was not planned. You may have made a mistake. God still loves you, and will never stop loving you. He has given life to your precious child. You don't have to be ashamed. He loves and accepts both of you unconditionally.

Or maybe you face a different scenario. You may have been told that there are serious problems with your child, and survival is slim. God has given life to your child. Your baby will be born, and she will be perfect.

And if you have a beautiful baby growing inside as you always wanted, acknowledge that God has given her life. He has blessed and created her to be a wonderful addition to your family.

Whatever your circumstance may be, God is the giver of life. He has given life to your baby.

Confession and prayer: Father God, thank You for giving life to my baby.

Week 15: Day 2

Ezekiel 19:2 (CEV) *Your mother was a brave lioness who raised her cubs among lions.*

Mothering is a huge job. The world is ever evolving and changing. The above verse talks of a mother, and likens her to a lioness. Mothers can be lionesses especially when it comes to protecting their little ones. Don't dare say anything bad about her child! However, Ezekiel's passage talks about a lioness in a slightly different way.

This lioness raised her children among lions. She was not overly protective. She raised children in the real world, and exposed them to the harshness of life. Don't be afraid of society, and how your child will respond. Raise your cub among the lions, because being a lion is her destiny.

At times, mothers can try to protect children from the culture they live in. Children certainly need protection, but they don't need smothering. Let them grow up among lions, and get roared at every now and again. Empower your children be all they can be, even if it means a few scars, and letting go along the way.

Confession and prayer: Father, help me to be the kind of mother You know my child needs. May I raise my cub to be a lion.

Week 15: Day 3

Psalm 78:6-7 (NLT) *So the next generation might know them—even the children not yet born—and they in turn will teach their own children. So each generation should set its hope anew on God, not forgetting his glorious miracles and obeying his commands.*

Have you ever taken the time to write down all the things God has done for you? Okay, let's narrow it down to the last twelve months. Think about all the wonderful things God has done for you in the last year. There's a lot, right?

God answers prayer, much more than we give Him credit for. We easily forget the good things He has done. But God does not want us to forget. He wants us to remember, never forget, and keep those memories in our mind. And He wants us to tell our children, even the ones not yet born.

God is good. The world will have you believe that God is angry and judgemental. Your children will grow up believing humanity's version of God, unless you tell them otherwise.

So while baby is in the womb, talk to her about God. Tell her all the good things He has done for you this year. Let her know that God is good to you and your family, continuing this practice for years to come.

Confession and prayer: God, You have done many good things for me this year. I am so thankful. I will tell my child of Your goodness in my life.

Week 15: Day 4

Psalm 34:11 (CEV) *Come, my children, listen as I teach you to respect the LORD.*

The single most important lesson for any child to learn is to honour God. It is not something they teach in schools anymore, but it is best taught at home anyway.

Your unborn child needs to know that God is deserving of honour and respect. He is our Creator and Saviour. He gave His life in place of ours. He is the reason we celebrate at Christmas and Easter. He is deserving of praise and worship.

Respecting God takes more than words. We honour the Lord by praying before we eat, attending church, giving offerings, and obeying His Word. With children, actions speak louder than words, so if you want them to honour God, make sure your actions do. And the earlier they learn to honour Him the better. Set good habits now.

Your child is like a sponge, soaking up all she can about life. Teach her to respect the Lord, and respecting others will come naturally.

Confession and prayer: I will teach my children to honour and respect the Lord. I will honour Him with my actions.

Week 15: Day 5

Psalm 118:6 (NKJV) *The Lord is on my side; I will not fear. What can man do to me?*

Isn't it good to know that God is on your side? Perhaps you are going against the wishes of your doctor and others by continuing your pregnancy. It may feel like no one is with you. Be encouraged today, God is on your side!

Elisha was surrounded by the army of Aram. They had come to destroy Him. Elisha's servant was full of fear. He thought they were doomed. But Elisha saw things differently. He knew that with God on their side, nothing could stand against them. Elisha prayed that his servant's eyes would be opened. When they were, the servant realised they were not forsaken. He saw a chariots of fire ready to battle for them.

If you feel abandoned and alone in your pregnancy, I pray that the eyes of your heart would be opened today. I pray that you will see that there are more for you than against you. You have nothing to fear. God is on your side.

Confession and prayer: Father, thank You for being on my side. Open my eyes to see those who are with me.

Week 15: Day 6

Malachi 2:15 (NLT) *Didn't the Lord make you one with your wife? In body and spirit you are his. And what does he want? Godly children from your union. So guard your heart; remain loyal to the wife of your youth.*

God says some strong things to His children in Malachi, one of them being this passage about marriage. God does not take marital union lightly. From the beginning of time, He designed marriage as a covenant relationship between man and woman. It is more than an institution.

One of the reasons God cares so much about marriage is because the result of marriage is children - godly children. Children who love Him, and will carry faith onto the next generation. When marriages are destroyed, producing godly children becomes harder. Not impossible, but harder.

As you prepare for the birth of this child, spend time on your marriage too. Have a few date nights, and get away together if you can. With a new baby, you probably won't get the chance for a while. Guard your heart against temptation, and remain faithful. Loving your spouse is a gift to your children, and a gift to Father.

Confession and prayer: Lord, I love my spouse. I guard my heart, and remain faithful to him always.

Week 15: Day 7

Psalm 128:3a (NLT) *Your wife will be like a fruitful grapevine, flourishing within your home.*

Fruitful and flourishing. The Lord desires that you be fruitful and flourishing in your home.

Some women find childbearing, and the weeks that follow, to be difficult. This may cause them to struggle bonding with their new baby, or battle depression. Depression is not flourishing. God's plan for you,as a mother, is to flourish.

If you have experienced postnatal depression in the past, do not feel condemned. However, claim that you will not experience that condition with this pregnancy. You don't need to fear what will happen once your child is born. You will bond with her, and love her. You will thrive with baby, and with the babies you already have.

You are an amazing, fruitful, and flourishing mother. God will help you through everything, so that you flourish within your home.

Confession and prayer: Lord, I accept Your destiny of being fruitful and flourishing. I do not accept depression in my life.

Week 16: Day 1

Psalm 128:3 (NLT) *Your wife will be like a fruitful grapevine, flourishing within your home. Your children will be like vigorous young olive trees as they sit around your table.*

What does a vigorous olive tree look like? Sometimes the descriptions of things in the Bible are interesting. We read a translation of the original, and sometimes there are no English words to capture what the author, and God, meant to say.

Whatever picture comes into your mind as your liken children to a vigorous olive tree, let us focus on the latter part of the Scripture: around your table. Children are successful as they sit around the family table.

These days, many families are too busy to sit and eat dinner together around the table. Some families don't even have a dining table, but eat in front of the television. Unfortunately, children will not thrive around the latest sitcom, they thrive as they interact with their parents and siblings around the family table.

Begin a habit of regularly having dinner around the table. Make this time a place where you talk with one another and share your lives. God promises that when children spend time around your table, they will be vigorous young olive trees. Whatever that means, it is good!

Confession and prayer: Lord, I will spend time with my family around the dinner table. Thank You that my children are thriving and successful.

Week 16: Day 2

Psalm 27:1 (NLT) *The Lord is my light and my salvation— so why should I be afraid? The Lord is my fortress, protecting me from danger, so why should I tremble?*

Have you found yourself feeling afraid lately? Have you worried about the world that you are bringing your child into? Have you been fearful that there may be something wrong with your baby? Have you been concerned about your financial situation? Hear this: The Lord is my light, salvation and fortress, why should I be afraid?

Whatever your worry, whatever your care, He is greater. The Lord is light in the dark situation you face. He has the power to rescue you from your problems. He is protecting you from all danger. You don't need to tremble.

When fear, worry, doubt, and anxiety attempt to overwhelm you, focus on The Lord, your Salvation. He will light the way, and get you through. He is your personal refuge and strength. Draw from Him. His power and might is never ending. He is Light in this dark world, and His light will dispel your fears.

Confession and prayer: God, I look to You, my light and salvation. I do not fear.

Week 16: Day 3

John 14:27 (NLT) *I am leaving you with a gift—peace of mind and heart. And the peace I give is a gift the world cannot give. So don't be troubled or afraid.*

It is always nice to receive a gift. Receiving gifts for celebrations like Christmas or birthdays is wonderful, but a gift "just because" is even more special. Just because I love you. Just because you did a great job. Just because I think you are amazing. Just because you are who you are. Those kinds of gifts are the ones that stand out, and make us feel incredible.

Father God has a gift for you today, just because. Just because He loves you. Just because you are His beloved child, and He cares for you. Just because you are His precious creation. And the gift? Peace. Peace of mind and heart. A peace that the world knows nothing about, and is unable to give. His peace. So don't be troubled or afraid.

Receive the Father's gift of peace in your life today. Allow it to flood your heart and overtake you. It is His "just because" gift for you. Peace that gives confidence, stillness, and time. Sense His peace in your life, and allow it to flow into those around you. Everyone needs more peace.

Confession and prayer: Lord, I receive Your gift of peace in my life today. Peace of heart and mind.

Week 16: Day 4

Deuteronomy 28:11 (NLT) *The Lord will give you prosperity in the land he swore to your ancestors to give you, blessing you with many children, numerous livestock, and abundant crops.*

Satan would like you to think that God is judging you, holding back from you, and will punish and abandon you the moment things go wrong. That is not the God of the Bible. He is a good God who longs to bless.

God desires to give His children what He promised. He promised the children of Israel they would live in a land to call their own after being slaves for four hundred years. And He did. He blessed their livestock and their crops so they were abundant. And they were. He blessed the people so they would multiply, and have many children. That is what happened.

God has not changed. In fact, because of Jesus, He has even more grace and blessing to shower upon you. You will have many children, and you will prosper. He will bless you so that you can be a blessing to others. Believe His Word. Believe His promises. They are yours for the taking.

Confession and prayer: God, I confess today that I am abundantly blessed. I have blessed children, a blessed career, and a blessed home.

Week 16: Day 5

Psalm 27:14 (NLT) *Wait patiently for the Lord. Be brave and courageous. Yes, wait patiently for the Lord.*

Now that you are roughly sixteen weeks pregnant, a bit of the excitement may have worn off, and you realise that forty weeks is quite a long way away. Being pregnant is all about waiting. If you weren't patient before, pregnancy will teach you patience.

Pregnancy is a time of joyful anticipation. Of discovering whether you are having a boy or a girl, what your child will be like, and how it will feel to be a parent. Because each child, and pregnancy, is different, these experiences are new for everyone. But you have to be patient. They will all come in good time.

Psalm 27 says to wait patiently for the Lord. He will bring all these amazing events, and more, to pass. You have to be patient. Wait on Him today, and allow God to develop the fourth fruit of the spirit in your life. As any parent will tell you, having children means being patient. Being pregnant is not even the half of it!

Confession and prayer: Lord, as I wait on You today, teach me patience. Develop Your patience in me.

Week 16: Day 6

2 Corinthians 12:9 (NLT) *Each time he said, "My grace is all you need. My power works best in weakness." So now I am glad to boast about my weaknesses, so that the power of Christ can work through me.*

Giving birth is daunting for many new parents. It can make some people feel weak and sick at the thought. But when you are feeling weak, God's power can work its best.

Baby's birth may seem like a long way away, but it is good to begin to meditate on the type of birth that God wants you to have. The first thing to recognise is that in your weakness, He is strong. Where you may be worried and unsure, rely on Him. If you are in pain and distressed, His power will work through you. His grace is all you need.

God promises that in our weakest moment, He will be strong. Birth is exhausting and emotionally draining. It can present the unexpected, and you may have to make life threatening decisions, while the world is spinning. In that moment, His grace is all you need. He will show Himself strong.

Throughout your pregnancy and birth, meditate on the Lord, your strength in times of weakness. See His grace working through you every step of the way.

Confession and prayer: Father, I meditate on Your power and grace. Thank You for being strength in my weakest moment.

Week 16: Day 7

Luke 1:24 (NLT) *Soon afterward his wife, Elizabeth, became pregnant and went into seclusion for five months.*

Elizabeth had wanted a child her whole life. Just when she thought that her time was over, God granted her request, and gave her a baby. And not just any baby, she raised a child who Jesus said was the greatest prophet of the Old Testament.

It is interesting that when Elizabeth found out she was pregnant; she went into seclusion for five months. Elizabeth understood the power of words. She knew that she could not stay around people who would fill her mind with doubt and worry. Instead she spent time in the presence of God, listening to His words.

God filled Elizabeth with faith and hope. He taught her how to mother one of the most significant men of God ever to walk the earth. He taught her to be an encouragement to others. She learnt to speak life and blessing. She learnt to speak favour and prophecy.

Elizabeth became a better woman as she spent time with God, and learnt to speak like Him. She became the mother we all aspire to.

Confession and prayer: Father, today I choose to spend time with You, learning to speak Your words in every situation.

Week 17: Day 1

Luke 1:20 (NLT) *"But now, since you didn't believe what I said, you will be silent and unable to speak until the child is born. For my words will certainly be fulfilled at the proper time."*

Perhaps Elizabeth knew the power of words through what happened to her husband. You see, when an angel appeared to Zechariah announcing that he would soon be a father, his response wasn't all joy and elation. He said, "How can I be sure this will happen? I'm an old man now, and my wife is also well along in years."

And with that, Zechariah could no longer speak. The birth of the child, who we know as John the Baptist, was too important. John had a job to do. God would not allow even one inch of doubt, unbelief, or fear to stop John from being born. The instant Zechariah uttered doubt, God shut his mouth.

Words are powerful. The words you speak about your baby are powerful: potent enough to affect her destiny. So speak words of life, hope, happiness, peace, and love over your child. Do not allow words of fear out of your mouth. Even in the womb, words will affect your child. Make sure they count for the best.

Confession and prayer: Father, I realise there is power in my words. I speak words of life, love, and hope over the child in my womb.

Hebrews 12:2a (NLT) *We do this by keeping our eyes on Jesus, the champion who initiates and perfects our faith.*

Keep your eyes on Jesus. In life, there are many distractions. People will let you down. Circumstances won't go the way you plan. Life will catch you off guard. At those times, other things can become the focus. But when we fix our eyes on Jesus, despite what is going on around us, there is a constant who will bring us through.

When the disciples were caught in a raging storm, they looked at the wind and waves, and were filled with fear. Then Jesus came walking through the storm. One person, Peter, was able to focus on Jesus. As long as he was fixated on Jesus, he could do the impossible. When his focus returned to the circumstance, he began to sink.

Where is your focus during pregnancy? You can focus on the circumstances, and things will probably continue as they have been, or get worse. Alternatively, you can focus on Jesus. He is your Source. He is your Healer. He is your Hope. He is your Life. Focus on Him, and you can do the impossible.

Confession and prayer: Jesus, I choose to focus on you. I will not let my eyes deviate.

Week 17: Day 3

1 John 5:14-15 (NLT) *And we are confident that he hears us whenever we ask for anything that pleases him. And since we know he hears us when we make our requests, we also know that he will give us what we ask for.*

Do you remember asking your parents for something special one Christmas? They may have told you things like, "You'll have to wait and see," but deep down you knew you would receive what you asked for. After all, your parents loved you, and wanted to give you your heart's desire.

Father God is even more eager to give you what you ask. When you pray to Him, you can be confident He hears. He is not asleep or busy. He is listening to every word you say.

Prayer is not as complex as some think or make out. It is as simple as ask, believe, receive. Ask God; believe He is listening and desires to answer; receive. The reason some prayers don't get answered is not because God is not listening, it is because we are not confident in Him. We are not certain He wants to answer. We are not sure we deserve to be answered. We are not expectant of His amazing love and goodness.

God is good and He answers prayer. When you approach Him, do it with confidence. He hears, and He answers. Whatever your prayer through pregnancy, be confident that it is answered.

Confession and prayer: Father, I am convinced You are a good God, and that You will answer my prayer.

Week 17: Day 4

Isaiah 41:10 (NLT) *Don't be afraid, for I am with you. Don't be discouraged, for I am your God. I will strengthen you and help you. I will hold you up with my victorious right hand.*

Today is a day of victory. You are a winner. God has come to your rescue. He is holding you up. The enemy is defeated. Don't be afraid or discouraged.

God is not propping you up. You aren't barely standing. He is your strength and help. Sorry to all the lefties out there, but right hands represent triumph. A warrior holds his sword in his right hand. He wields his sword with skill and punishes the enemy. God's hand of might and power is upon you. Be assured that you will not fail.

If your current situation is making you fearful, discouraged, or weary, look to the Lord. He is your rescuer. He is holding you up with His right hand. Believe His Word, and receive His strength, help, and victory. If pregnancy is wearing you out, tap into Him. Success, triumph, power, courage, and help are yours.

Confession and prayer: God, I receive Your victory in my life. Thank You for upholding me with Your right hand.

Week 17: Day 5

Zephaniah 3:17 (NLT) *For the Lord your God is living among you. He is a mighty savior. He will take delight in you with gladness. With his love, he will calm all your fears. He will rejoice over you with joyful songs.*

Beautiful baby, the Lord is living among you. He is a mighty saviour. He takes delight in your gladness. With His love, He will calm any and all your fears. He will rejoice over you, sweet child, with joyful songs.

Precious one, Your God will never leave you or forsake you. He will be at your side, among you, like a friend. He is your ever protector, especially when mummy and daddy can't be around.

Jesus is happy when you are happy. He loves to see you enjoy life, and the world He made. He creates situations to make you feel special and loved by Him.

And my darling, whenever you are afraid, Jesus will calm your fears with love. His love will make fear melt because the love of God is more powerful than anything on the planet.

At night, when mummy and daddy have put you to sleep, listen carefully. Because in that moment, you will hear your Heavenly Father rejoice over you with singing. He will sing you sweet lullabies to put you to sleep.

Never forget how much your Creator loves you.

Confession and prayer: God, Your love for my child amazes me. You rejoice over her with singing.

Week 17: Day 6

Isaiah 32:17 (NLT) *And this righteousness will bring peace. Yes, it will bring quietness and confidence forever.*

By now, you have probably had a few well meaning people tell you things about pregnancy. It was most likely based on their experience, giving you an idea of what to expect. The problem is that what they told you does not line up with what you have read in the Bible.

If you are a believer in the finished work of the Cross of Christ, you have been made the righteousness of God. According to Isaiah, that righteousness in your life brings peace. Peace that things will go your way. That everything will work out.

Being the righteousness of God entitles you to everything God has promised in the Word. He has promised health, wholeness, and redemption from the curse. People may tell you how painful giving birth can be, but you don't have to accept that in your life. You can have peace that despite the struggles others have had, your experiences will be different.

Explaining what you believe to some is no use. Instead, smile and have quiet confidence. Rest in His righteousness, and allow serenity and conviction to override whatever is said that does not agree with the Word of God. Yes, the righteousness of Jesus in your life will bring peace, quietness, and confidence forever.

Confession and prayer: Lord, I have a quiet confidence in the promises you have given me about my baby and birth.

Week 17: Day 7

Isaiah 26:3 (NLT) *You will keep in perfect peace all who trust in you, all whose thoughts are fixed on you!*

Fix your thoughts today on things above. That is the key to living a peaceful life. If you need more peace (or just some peace full stop), focus on Jesus. Meditate on Him and His Word. That is where true tranquility comes from.

Being overwhelmed at work, screaming children, a strained marriage, or struggles with your pregnancy, may cause you to lose peace. Jesus is the answer. Stop thinking about the problem, start thinking about Him. Thinking about the situation will only make you lose sleep. Thinking about Jesus will endow calmness.

God does not want you stressed. It is not good for you or your child. His peace is there for you. Center your thoughts on Him throughout the day. Let His perfect peace fill your life. Let His perfect peace fill your womb. Let His perfect peace fill your baby. Trust in Jesus, He is your peace.

Confession and prayer: Jesus, I allow Your peace to fill my heart, mind, body, womb, and baby. I focus my thoughts on You.

Week 18: Day 1

Psalm 16:11 (NLT) *You will show me the way of life, granting me the joy of your presence and the pleasures of living with you forever.*

God is there. Very present in your situation. You can't get away from Him. Whether you want Him to be or not. His presence surrounds, bringing joy and pleasure.

The Lord's presence is at hand for you and baby. He is in the womb with her, watching as her body takes shape. She is not alone or rejected. He shows her the way of life.

Think of a time in your life when you felt the presence of the Lord, when you felt His nearness and touch. Tell baby about this experience. Explain to her that she has the presence of God with her in the same way. Encourage her to sense Him, and be aware of Him. To enjoy the pleasure of His company, as she bathes in the presence of God in the womb. And while you are at it, you might want to do the same. Experience the wonder of His presence, and the ecstasy of living with Him forever.

Confession and prayer: God, let Your presence fill my baby today. I bathe in the solace of Your habitation.

Week 18: Day 2

James 1:4 (NLT) *So let it grow, for when your endurance is fully developed, you will be perfect and complete, needing nothing.*

Many of baby's organs are already fully developed. Her facial features and physical traits are taking shape. In the next few days, your will have a morphology scan, and catch a glimpse of what she looks like. It is amazing to know there are resemblances between the images in the scan, and the baby you will see when she is born months later.

Now is the time to relax and let her grow. Then, at the right time, when she is fully developed, she will be born, perfect and complete, needing nothing. What a beautiful promise.

Being able to see baby in utero is a wonderful advancement of science. Whether you are given a good report or not, hold to this verse. See your baby growing and developing so that when she is born, she will be whole and lacking nothing. That is God's promise to you.

Confession and prayer: Father, I believe my baby is growing, and at the right time, she will be born perfect, needing nothing.

Week 18: Day 3

Isaiah 43:1 (NIV) *But now, this is what the Lord says—he who created you, Jacob,*
he who formed you, Israel: "Do not fear, for I have redeemed you; I have summoned you by name; you are mine.

Baby, your Father in Heaven wants to tell you something. He created you in the depths of my womb. He made your spirit, soul, and body. He constructed your organs. He placed bones in order. You are fearfully and wonderfully made.

He formed the shape of your face: lips, eyes, nose; all a perfect fit for you. He shaped even the smallest part of you: your fingernails and eyelashes. You have lovely fingers, and cute toes because God made them so.

You are redeemed, my child, with the precious Blood of Jesus. No sin, sickness, or strife can get the better of you when you call on His Name. Your Redeemer lives.

And, my precious one, God calls you by name. He has a divine plan for your life. You are called to live at this time, and for His purpose. You are, and always will be, His. His eyes are on you. You are forever on His mind.

Confession and prayer: God, You made my baby, called her, and formed her. She is Yours, always and ever.

Week 18: Day 4

Psalm 4:8 (NLT) *In peace I will lie down and sleep, for you alone, O Lord, will keep me safe.*

If you are a first time parent, blissful sleep rituals will soon change. Even if you have other children, a new baby will make things a little more interesting.

When children are waking up through the night, the last thing you need is to lie awake worrying about things. Sleep is precious. It helps you cope, and decreases the likelihood of depression. So before you go to sleep at night, get in the habit of reciting this Scripture. God has peaceful sleep for you, sleeping in His safety and protection.

Not only that, God has peaceful sleep for your entire family, especially your new baby. As you pray for your child, believe that she will have peaceful slumber. Your baby will be a good sleeper, and will wake happy and refreshed. She is learning sleep patterns as she is in the womb. Tell her she is a good sleeper. Confess it over her often. Everyone functions better with sleep.

Confession and prayer: Father, I believe You have peaceful sleep for me, and my entire family, especially the baby in my womb.

Week 18: Day 5

2 Peter 1:5-7 (NLT) *In view of all this, make every effort to respond to God's promises. Supplement your faith with a generous provision of moral excellence, and moral excellence with knowledge, and knowledge with self-control, and self-control with patient endurance, and patient endurance with godliness, and godliness with brotherly affection, and brotherly affection with love for everyone.*

God has made promises about having children and prospering as a family. Here, Peter explains our response to His promises. Many people think the response to God's promises is to name it and claim it. However, according to Peter, we respond to God's promises by developing godly character.

You are claiming promises from the Word about your child, and you should. Keep meditating on His promises, and believing you already have them. That is how you receive. But don't neglect things like living a moral life, exercising self control, and showing love and grace to others.

God is concerned with the growth and development of your baby right now, but He is also concerned with your spiritual growth. He loves you like a child, and is pleased when you choose to live according to His ways. Life is better when we are controlled, patient, godly, and show love to one another. Respond to His promises by developing godly character.

Confession and prayer: Lord, I respond to your promises by developing Your character, and living a holy life.

Week 18: Day 6

John 16:33 (NLT) *I have told you all this so that you may have peace in me. Here on earth you will have many trials and sorrows. But take heart, because I have overcome the world.*

Jesus is an overcomer. He overcame death, sickness, poverty, lack, strife, stress, and more when He died on the Cross. There is nothing that Jesus has not overcome.

By believing that Jesus Christ is the Son of God, and that He died for your sin, you take part in the victory He purchased. Which means, you are an overcomer too. You have overcome whatever trials and sorrows you may face.

If you are experiencing testing times in your pregnancy or life today, know that you are an overcomer. Situations will not overwhelm you because you conquer. The enemy is defeated. See yourself joining Jesus in His triumphant parade over the enemy.

Here on this earth we will all experience trials and sorrows from time to time. As a believer in Jesus, you can take heart in spite of trials. Why? Because in the end, you will overcome the world with Jesus.

Confession and prayer: Jesus, thank You for making me an overcomer.

Romans 8:6b (NLT) *Letting the Spirit control your mind leads to life and peace.*

There is a saying that you are what you eat. More accurate would be, "You are what you think." As Proverbs tells us, "As a man thinks in his heart, so is he." What have you been thinking about lately? Who has been controlling your mind? The Spirit or the world?

Are you meditating on what God says about your baby, or are you worried that your child could be born with a defect or illness? Are you worried and stressed, or content with life? Do you have a short fuse at the moment, or are you fun to be around? Does your life look like life and peace, or worry, arguments, and sickness?

If your answers are the wrong side of those questions, the problem begins with the mind, and who is controlling it. If you need the Spirit to take more control, pray, and ask Him to. When thoughts wander toward negativity, switch your thinking to that of the Spirit. His thoughts are those of love, joy, peace, patience, gentleness, goodness, faithfulness, kindness, and self-control.

Pregnant mothers are best when they are peaceful, so let the Spirit control your mind. Both you and baby will benefit from a Spirit-led life.

Confession and prayer: Holy Spirit, control my mind today so that I experience God's life and peace.

Week 19: Day 1

Ecclesiastes 11:10 (NLT) *So refuse to worry, and keep your body healthy.*

It seems that you can't do much these days without being told to eat well, exercise more, and live a healthy lifestyle. Our world is not just health conscious, but in many ways, health obsessed. The Bible also has a few things to say about being healthy. One tip is found in Ecclesiastes - don't worry. Actually, the Bible says refuse to worry. You see, worrying is a choice. You allow yourself to worry, or you can refuse it place in your life.

Most mothers want to keep in shape while pregnant. You might be watching what you eat, and doing light exercise. You have possibly read about, and are implementing, the right foods and nutrients to eat so that you and baby have strong bodies. Another item to add to the list is to refuse to worry. Stop giving time to this type of oppression. It is a waste. Most of what you concern yourself with, will not happen.

Being worry free is good for you and baby. Babies in the womb pick up on stress. Your child does not need to experience anxiety, and neither do you. Because you are a mother it does not mean you should be a worrier. Well, wouldn't you like it if your mother worried less!

Confession and prayer: God, I refuse to worry. It will not occupy time in my day.

Week 19: Day 2

Joshua 1:9 (NLT) *This is my command—be strong and courageous! Do not be afraid or discouraged. For the Lord your God is with you wherever you go.*

Pregnancy is a nine month journey. You will encounter new emotions, and experiences along the way. What lies ahead may be exciting, yet daunting. God says, "Be strong and courageous." Go forward confidently. You have nothing to fear.

It has been said before, but every pregnancy is different. Despite what you have experienced in the past, the future is unknown. The good news is that God is the same, yesterday, today, and forever. He has been with you in the past, and He will be with you in the future. Even better, He knows what the future holds. He knows what will happen during this last half of your pregnancy. He knows what will happen during your baby's birth. His command remains the same, "Be strong and courageous."

The Lord your God is with you while you are expecting. You will not be harmed or suffer loss. Go forth, strong and courageous, confident that you will receive all He has promised to you.

Confession and prayer: Lord, I decide that I will be strong and courageous in my pregnancy.

Week 19: Day 3

Ephesians 5:29a (NLT) *No one hates his own body but feeds and cares for it.*

When you are pregnant, often your focus, and that of those around you, shifts to the little one you carry. Everything you do is done with her in mind. While that is certainly a good thing, may I also encourage you to love and care for your own body during your pregnancy.

Sharing your body with another human being is hard work. It will knock your body around. You will not bounce back to normal once you have given birth, despite the celebrity photos you see. And baby always get the best. Our bodies were designed to give the growing baby the best nutrients, and will allow baby to grow perfectly at all costs. Mum gets whatever is left over.

Your body is automatically looking after baby, that is why you need to purposefully look after yourself. Are you getting enough sleep? Are you exercising? Are you eating well? Make time for yourself. Do some of the things you like. Get a massage, catch up with friends, go shopping, not for the baby, but for you. Don't feel guilty, you'll soon lose the opportunity for "me" time. Looking after yourself is a good thing. And in reality, the person to benefit from it most, will be baby.

Confession and prayer: I will look after my body and care for myself.

Week 19: Day 4

Genesis 25:22a (CEV) *Before Rebekah gave birth, she knew she was going to have twins, because she could feel them inside her, fighting each other.*

One of the best experiences is feeling your baby's movements in utero. The kicks, hiccups, and sometimes tumble turns, are precious and amazing. If this is your first pregnancy, you probably felt movement, but were unsure whether it was baby, your aorta, or imagination. By now though, the moves are distinguishable. They will intensify in the coming months.

Each time you feel baby kick and move, pray for her. Thank God for her precious limbs that are learning how to operate in the womb. Praise Him for a strong and active baby. Pray her body will not be affected by birth, and that she will develop adequate motor skills. See her running, kicking, reaching, and touching.

Just as Rebekah felt her babies movement, take pleasure in the kicks and nudges - - little reminder of baby's presence everywhere you go. Enjoy these beautiful sensations because when they are gone, they're gone.

Confession and prayer: Lord, I treasure each time my baby moves. I pray she will be a strong and active child.

Week 19: Day 5

Proverbs 3:7-8 (NLT) *Don't be impressed with your own wisdom. Instead, fear the Lord and turn away from evil. Then you will have healing for your body and strength for your bones.*

There are many educated and intelligent people on the planet. The big words they use, and all the letters after their names, sound impressive. God is not impressed by such things. He says that we shouldn't be overawed with our own wisdom, but instead, worship The Lord, and turn from evil. Then we will find healing for our bodies, and strength for our bones.

If you need healing in your body, medical science will help. But the wisdom to seek first, is God's wisdom found in His Word. His wisdom is superior to the understanding of the world. God's wisdom will heal, and bring strength to your bones.

If you or baby need healing or strength, don't be impressed, or intimidated, by man's intelligence. Healing and strength will come to you as you fear the Lord, and turn from evil. Mediate on His wisdom, and let it come first in your life.

Confession and prayer: Lord, I am not impressed by man's wisdom. I rely on the wisdom of Your Word for healing in my body, and strength to my bones.

Week 19: Day 6

Psalm 71:17 (NLT) *O God, you have taught me from my earliest childhood, and I constantly tell others about the wonderful things you do.*

By now, baby's nervous system is developing nicely and she can taste, smell, touch, hear, and see. There could even be some hair sprouting from her little head. There is so much going on physically, that we forget she has a spirit, learning and growing as well. As it tells us in Psalm 71, Father God is teaching baby's spirit while she is in the womb, and has been for some time.

Children have such sweet, innocent souls. They soak up each moment, and learn from every experience. Before the world has a chance to corrupt them, babies spend nine months in the womb learning from God. How precious!

When your child is born, keep talking to her about the things of God. Expose her to worship music and Bible stories. You will find her spirit catches on quickly because she has already been taught by God Himself. You are simply building on the foundation He laid when He had her undivided attention.

Confession and prayer: Lord, it is so precious that You are teaching my child. I pray she will always speak of Your goodness.

Week 19: Day 7

Philippians 4:13 (NLT) *For I can do everything through Christ, who gives me strength.*

You are almost half way through your pregnancy. How exciting! You are just over twenty weeks away from giving birth to a beautiful baby. The birthing process may seem daunting, and even scary. Don't be overwhelmed. You can start getting ready for giving birth to your child by confessing this Scripture: I can do all things through Christ who gives me strength.

You are a strong and capable woman. You have overcome your fears in previous situations. You have conquered doubts, and experienced success in the face of adversity. No obstacle is too great for you.

Whether your birthing experience goes exactly to plan, or nothing turns out as you hoped, God has given you all the strength you need to deal with the situation, and come through smiling. Keep confessing and believing that you can do all things, even the unexpected, because Jesus Christ gives you strength. Each time you think about giving birth remember, you are a strong and capable woman who can do all things through Christ.

Confession and prayer: I am a strong and capable woman. I can do all things through Christ who gives me strength.

Week 20: Day 1

Philippians 4:7a (NLT) *Then you will experience God's peace, which exceeds anything we can understand.*

Peace is more than a feeling, it is an experience. The Bible says that when you experience God's peace, it surpasses anything you can understand. Stop looking for a feeling, and go for the experience.

God's peace will overwhelm you and your situation. Confusion, doubts, and uneasiness will disappear. You will be filled with hope, faith, and confidence. The load will be easy. His peace will follow you all day and into the night. You will have restful sleep. The Lord's peace is not fleeting, it endures. It is serenity beyond explanation. That is the peace experience.

God wants you to experience His peace in your pregnancy. Peace that passes all understanding. Peace that baby is alright. Peace that you will not just cope, but thrive in your new role as a mother. Peace that whatever the future holds, you rest in the loving arms of your Saviour. Jesus is your peace. Experience Him.

Confession and prayer: Lord, I want to experience Your peace today.

Week 20: Day 2

Philippians 4:7b (NLT) *His peace will guard your hearts and minds as you live in Christ Jesus.*

Yesterday we spoke about experiencing God's peace. Today we see that His peace is not merely an experience, but it produces results - peace guards hearts and minds.

The experience of God's peace is robbed so easily. Everyday worries and doubts push it out of our lives, replacing peace with fear and confusion. God's peace often leaves so subtly that we don't even notice. But when the experience of peace is gone, stress and confusion quickly become the reality.

The way to be sure that you continue in Christ's peace experience, is to see if your life is producing the right results. Are your hearts and minds guarded? In a stressful situation, do you remain calm, assured of God's promises? Regardless of the situation, is your mind and heart fixed on His Word? Then peace is reigning in your life, and guarding your heart and mind from any attacks. Practically, this is quite difficult.

Allow yourself to experience God's peace, and let it guard your heart and mind today, and every day.

Confession and prayer: Lord, let Your peace guard my heart and mind in every situation.

Week 20: Day 3

Deuteronomy 30:9 (NLT) *The Lord your God will then make you successful in everything you do. He will give you many children and numerous livestock, and he will cause your fields to produce abundant harvests, for the Lord will again delight in being good to you as he was to your ancestors.*

You are a child of Abraham. Perhaps you sang a song about it as a child. Abraham is your distant relative. God took delight in being good to Abraham. He loved to bless Abraham and caused him to increase in every area of his life.

God blessed Abraham and made him successful. He was wealthy with many servants, and a growing business. Eventually, God also blessed Abraham with the children he longed for. Abraham prospered because the Lord took delight in being good to him.

As Abraham's child, God will take delight in being good to you. He has blessed you with the child in your womb. He also wants to bless you in other areas: your finances, marriage, relationships, health, and emotions. God is not an either or God. He longs to be good to you in every part of your life. Do not settle for lack in any area. It is Father's delight to be good to you.

Confession and prayer: God, I accept Your goodness in every part of my life today, especially in my pregnancy.

Week 20: Day 4

Luke 1:15 (NLT) *For he will be great in the eyes of the Lord. He must never touch wine or other alcoholic drinks. He will be filled with the Holy Spirit, even before his birth.*

Your child can be filled with the Holy Spirit even before her birth. She can experience the anointing of God on her life in a powerful way in the womb. God's hand is on her. She will be great in His eyes.

This passage is of course talking of John the Baptist. John's birth was miraculous, and due to divine intervention. He was set apart for the Lord even before conception. John had a job to do. He prepared the way for the earthly ministry of Jesus. He was the greatest of all Old Testament prophets.

But Jesus said that believers, and participants of His new kingdom, would be greater than John the Baptist. This is why I can say that God wants to fill your child with the Holy Spirit in the womb. If God did it for John, of course are wants to do it for those who come after Him.

Lay your hands on your stomach and pray over your baby. Pray that she will be filled with the Holy Spirit in the womb, and that she will be great, and do awesome works for the Lord. Pray she will feel His presence and anointing, even in the womb.

Confession and prayer: As I lay hands on my womb, I believe that You are filling her with the Holy Spirit. May she be great in Your sight.

Week 20: Day 5

Romans 12:2 (NLT) *Don't copy the behavior and customs of this world, but let God transform you into a new person by changing the way you think. Then you will learn to know God's will for you, which is good and pleasing and perfect.*

According to the behaviours and customs of this world, pregnancy is uncomfortable, and giving birth is a screaming fest - yet somehow remarkably tidy and modest. You can listen to and believe the horror stories, or you can let God change the way you think about giving birth. He has a different kind of normal, that is yours if you want to experience it.

When Eve was created, she was made pain free. Her body was never supposed to experience pain. Once sin entered the world, women received a curse that they would experience pain in childbirth. That's where all the screaming comes from. When Jesus came, He redeemed the earth of every curse that was placed upon it. Women have been redeemed from the curse of experiencing pain in childbirth.

God wants to change your mind about childbirth. He never designed your body to experience pain giving birth. It is not His will for you. By meditating on the Word and His ways, you can experience a new kind of normal. No pain, no screaming, no complications, and no death. That is His good and pleasing will for your body.

Confession and prayer: I allow God to change the way I think about pregnancy and birth, so that I can do what is good and pleasing to Him and my body that He made.

Week 20: Day 6

2 Timothy 1:5 (NLT) *I remember your genuine faith, for you share the faith that first filled your grandmother Lois and your mother, Eunice. And I know that same faith continues strong in you.*

The Bible talks a lot about generations. Our Father is the God of Abraham, Isaac, and Jacob. His desire is that whole households and families are saved. God celebrates families where generations follow Him, as He did in the life of Timothy.

You see, when generations of people are believers, the younger generations are able to build on what has gone before. They don't have to face the same battles and struggles of the past generation, but can take new ground and go to new heights. This was the case in the life of Timothy. He was young, and yet he was a great pastor, because he was building on the faith of his mother and grandmother.

Decide that your child will serve the Lord. Pray she will do greater things in her walk with God than you. Do everything you can to give her grounding in living a Kingdom life. Let your faith continue strong in her life.

Confession and prayer: Jesus,I want my child to know You. May she achieve greater things in Your Kingdom, than I.

Week 20: Day 7

1 Samuel 12:7 (NLT) *Now stand here quietly before the Lord as I remind you of all the great things the Lord has done for you and your ancestors.*

When was the last time you stood quietly? In our world, quiet moments are few and far between. Today, God wants you to come before Him and be quiet. That's right, He doesn't want you to say a thing. Instead, let Him speak to you. He wants to remind you of all the good things he has done for you and your ancestors.

Take thirty minutes today to sit with God. Have pen and paper (iPad or notebook) at the ready, and let Him remind you of what He has done. Let Him remind you of the things we often gloss over, the things you probably haven't thanked Him for yet. You have much to be grateful for.

The devil would have us think that good fortune in life is due to coincidence, luck, and chance. You fell pregnant because you were lucky. No, you fell pregnant because God made it possible. He has worked on purpose in your life placing you where you are today. Let Him reveal when you have experienced His goodness, and then your eyes will be more aware of it in the future.

Confession and prayer: Lord, I quiet myself to listen to Your voice. Reveal to me Your blessing and goodness in my life.

Week 21: Day 1

Psalm 13:5 (NLT) *But I trust in your unfailing love. I will rejoice because you have rescued me.*

God loves you. His love is never ending, never failing, and never ceasing. You may have heard the words, "I love you," only to find that the love was imperfect and incomplete. Jesus Christ is not like that. You can trust Him, and His love for you and your child.

Hopefully you have a loving and Christ centred relationship with your baby's father. But perhaps for a few, that is not the case. The love in the relationship failed. You and baby have a Father in Heaven who will not just replace that love, but surpass it. His love for you and baby will never end. It is perfect and complete.

You and baby are loved and adored. You are secure and safe in the arms of the God of Ages. He will not let you go without. He will provide for your every need. Jesus will always be there for baby, like He is there for you. Rest and rejoice in the unfailing love of the Father.

Confession and prayer: God, thank You for Your never ending love. Others may let me down, but I know You will always love me, and my child.

Week 21: Day 2

Psalm 90:16 (NLT) *Let us, your servants, see you work again; let our children see your glory.*

The earthly ministry of Jesus was characterised by signs and wonders. Jesus accomplished many miracles that changed people's lives for the better. He performed the supernatural, seeing all who came to Him healed.

The prayer of many today is that we will see more signs and wonders. That God will once again demonstrate His power in our time. I long to see the power of Jesus operate among my peers, but as a parent, my desire to see Him manifest in my children's generation is even stronger. I pray that my children will see God's glory in a greater way, and in more power than I ever did.

It is not too early to start praying for your children and their generation. Oh, that they will experience His glory. That the Holy Spirit will manifest in power and might. That they will see signs and wonders, that bring many to salvation. God, show our children your glory.

Confession and prayer: Father, I pray that my child will experience and behold Your glory, in her life.

Week 21: Day 3

1 Samuel 2:1 (NLT) *My heart rejoices in the Lord! The Lord has made me strong. Now I have an answer for my enemies; I rejoice because you rescued me.*

This is the prayer of joy and thankfulness that Hannah prayed as she dedicated Samuel to the Lord. Hannah was unable to conceive a child until the Lord performed a miracle for her. After Samuel was born, Hannah had much to be thankful for. She rejoiced in the Lord, and proclaimed His goodness.

In Hannah's prayer we see a principle we too can apply – the principle of joyfulness. Live a life of rejoicing and gladness. Look on the bright side. Find satisfaction in little miracles and blessings. The funny thing about rejoicing is it makes you strong. This is what Hannah discovered. The joy of the Lord is your strength. Some think that challenges make you stronger. The Bible does not say that. Instead, God teaches that enjoying life makes you strong.

If you want to be strong as you deliver baby, don't focus on the challenge, rejoice! Over the next twenty weeks or so, rejoice at every opportunity, knowing that all the while you are building strength - strength you need for a safe and prosperous delivery.

Confession and prayer: Father, my heart rejoices in the Lord. Thank You for making me strong for the delivery of my child.

Week 21: Day 4

1 Peter 3:4 (NLT) *You should clothe yourselves instead with the beauty that comes from within, the unfading beauty of a gentle and quiet spirit, which is so precious to God.*

Nothing seems to fit, blotchy skin, and stretch marks. That pregnant glow? I don't think so! It can be difficult feeling, let alone looking, beautiful while you are pregnant. To make things worse, celebrity mums on the cover of magazines seem to do it in style, and hardly gain a kilo. If only...

But God sees things differently. First, know that Father thinks you are beautiful. He loves you the way you are, and can't get enough of you. He not only thinks you are beautiful physically, but He also sees your heart. He sees the beauty within. That is the kind of beauty He wants you to cultivate.

You may not feel all that glamorous on the outside at the moment, but know that to Father, you are. You have the unfading beauty of a gentle spirit. Let the beauty that is within rise today, because that is the true pregnant glow.

Confession and prayer: Lord, I know that you see me as beautiful. Help me develop inner beauty during my pregnancy.

Week 21: Day 5

Philippians 2:18 (NLT) *Yes, you should rejoice, and I will share your joy.*

The birth of a child is a joyous occasion. Those who love you and your family, will want to celebrate with you and be glad. What they often don't realise is that their presence takes precious time away from you and baby. Time that you want to bond and get to know her.

You know your family best. They will want to share your joy and spend time with your new baby. But remember she is that, your baby. What you want, and how much time you want alone with her, is your decision.

No one wants family conflict when a new baby has been born. It is a happy occasion. Take your family before the Lord. Pray about what you would like. If you feel you need to explain your wishes with your family, pray about the best way to do this so that feelings aren't hurt.

Share your baby, and may The Lord make it joyful for everyone.

Confession and prayer: Father, you know my family, and how they will respond to my baby. Show me the best way to share our joy so that everyone is glad.

Week 21: Day 6

Psalm 16:9 (NLT) *No wonder my heart is glad, and I rejoice. My body rests in safety.*

Are you feeling happy yet? God has been sending a pretty strong message lately - rejoice! So if you haven't started doing so, get happy. Be glad. Put a smile on your face. Laugh even. Or better yet, go to bed!

The promise of this verse is that your body rests in safety. And if your body rests in safety, then so does baby. Her body rests in safety too. What a great assurance.

Rest may be something that is eluding you of late. If that is the case, remember, it is important to look after yourself. It is not selfish, but you are caring for another as well. When you rest, she rests. The coming months will produce added strain and pressure. Relax while you can.

If you're not feeling happy at the moment, perhaps it's time to rest. Your baby, and body, will rejoice when you do.

Confession and prayer: Lord, my body rests safely in You, and I rejoice.

Week 21: Day 7

Deuteronomy 6:6-7 (NLT) *And you must commit yourselves wholeheartedly to these commands that I am giving you today. Repeat them again and again to your children. Talk about them when you are at home and when you are on the road, when you are going to bed and when you are getting up.*

Being a believer is more than attending church, saying a prayer when you need, or reading a few verses from the Bible. It's a lifestyle. This is what Deuteronomy teaches. Living for Jesus envelopes everything you do - sitting at home, walking around, driving, going to bed, getting up, and everything in between.

Not only is it your lifestyle, but it should be the lifestyle of your family. A normal Christian family should talk about God and the Bible all the time. In fact, it should be what they talk about most. Over and over again. This is what Moses was teaching the children of Israel. If you want to live for the Lord, He must be part of your everyday conversation.

Make an effort to talk with your family today about the things of God. And tomorrow, and the next day. Soon, you will find it very natural to talk about Him while you're shopping, driving, or simply doing life. That is a characteristic of a godly family.

Confession and prayer: I decide to get in the habit of talking with my family about the Bible, and what God is doing in all our lives.

Week 22: Day 1

Psalm 62:5 (NLT) *Let all that I am wait quietly before God, for my hope is in him.*

Our world tends to be noisy. Soon baby will experience and contribute to her noisy environment, but right now the sounds she hears are muted. She can hear the sound of your heartbeat, your voice, and that of those around you. For the most part, her world is quiet and peaceful. She is living this verse as she waits quietly before God for her time to be born.

There is a time for your child to be born. I will not be a moment too soon. Believe that your child will carry until full term. If there is a history of premature birth in your family, speak to your baby. Tell her to wait quietly before the Lord. If your family history is the opposite, in other words, children arrive late, speak to yourself. Tell yourself to wait quietly for your baby. Don't worry or try to make things happen. There is an appointed time for baby to be born. It is useless to hurry things along.

Whatever happens, pray that baby will be born when she is healthy and strong. Whenever that may be, both you and baby need to wait quietly before the Lord.

Confession and prayer: I confess that both baby and I will wait quietly before the Lord, so she is born at the appointed time.

Week 22: Day 2

Colossians 3:15 (NLT) *And let the peace that comes from Christ rule in your hearts. For as members of one body you are called to live in peace. And always be thankful.*

Is peace ruling in your life? What happens when you get a negative report? Or when you think you haven't felt baby move for a few days? Do you panic? Sleepless nights? Then peace isn't ruling, fear is. To have peace rule in your heart is a conscious choice. It is not something that just happens. You give peace permission to rule. You decide to let it take control.

Colossians shares how to make it easier for our lives to be ruled by peace. Firstly, it is the body of Christ collectively that has been called to peace. Experiencing God's peace in your life is easier when you hang around a body of believers who have a revelation of His peace. Go to a good church, and develop friendships with people of love, faith, and peace.

Secondly, be thankful. When your mind begins to worry, stop, and be thankful. I know that is easier said than done, but meditating on the good things God has done will leave you feeling peaceful. Be thankful for baby. Be thankful for your spouse, thankful for family, and friends who are a great support. Thankfulness makes peace the ruler of your heart.

Confession and prayer: I let peace rule in my heart, and I am thankful.

Week 22: Day 3

Psalm 139:14 (NLT) *Thank you for making me so wonderfully complex!*
Your workmanship is marvellous—how well I know it.

Reading the above verse you may be thinking that today I am going to address the marvellous creation of your baby. No, today, the focus is on you. Yes, you. You need to praise God for making you so marvellous and wonderful.

At roughly twenty-two weeks pregnant you are probably not thinking that your body looks all that wonderful. You have a round tummy, and perhaps a few more kilos than you'd like. And things are only going to get worse. Your tummy will get bigger, and there is a chance that some of the bodily changes you have experienced are irreversible.

Even so, God sees you as His marvellous workmanship. He loves your incredibly complex, pregnant body, inside and out. He is pleased with what He sees when He looks at you.

So go ahead, look in the mirror. Admire your fearfully and wonderfully made body. Delight in the changes pregnancy has made, and praise the Lord. You have been fearfully and beautifully made by your Creator at every stage of life.

Confession and prayer: Father, I delight in my pregnant (and even post pregnant) body. I am wonderfully made.

Week 22: Day 4

2 Corinthians 10:5 (NIV) *We demolish arguments and every pretension that sets itself up against the knowledge of God, and we take captive every thought to make it obedient to Christ.*

Even the most positive and upbeat person has thoughts of doubt and negativity appear in her head from time to time. For example, even the strongest of women will have thoughts such as, "What if my baby is born with a disability?" Or, "What if my baby experiences complications during birth and dies?"

It is in those times that you quickly take thoughts captive, and make them obedient to Christ. In other words, you immediately stop thinking that way, and think a thought that is in line with the Word of God. After all, the knowledge of God is whatever the Word says.

So instead of thinking, "What if my baby is born with a disability," you think, "My baby is fearfully and wonderfully made." Rather than thinking, "What if my baby dies during birth?" Think, "My baby will not die but live to declare the goodness of God."

Random, negative, and worrying thoughts pop into everyone's head. But you don't have to accept them, or agree with them. Take those thoughts captive, and make your mind obedient to what God says in the Bible.

Confession and prayer: God, whenever a negative thought pops into my head, I choose to take that thought captive. When I think about my baby and pregnancy, I only think things that are obedient to the Word of God.

Week 22: Day 5

Proverbs 5:18 (NLT) *Let your wife be a fountain of blessing for you. Rejoice in the wife of your youth.*

How is your relationship with your husband lately? Would you say that he is rejoicing in the wife of his youth? Or perhaps a better question is, are you being the kind of wife that brings her husband happiness?

During pregnancy, the focus is often on mum and the baby. A man can be made to feel left out, even by his very own wife.

The most important relationship that a wife has is with her husband. The Bible says that a woman should be a fountain of blessing to him. Fountains never run dry, instead they continually overflow. They are not draining, demanding, or absorbed in their own needs.

Every woman wants a man who dotes over her and is head over heels in love - a man who looks at her in the giddy way that he did when they were courting. Be a fountain of love, beauty, and joy to your husband. Be the woman that captivates his heart. Let him rejoice over you, and that he married you.

Confession and prayer: I decide to be a fountain of love and blessing to my husband. We are more in love today than when we first met.

Week 22: Day 6

Isaiah 14:7 (NLT) *But finally the earth is at rest and quiet. Now it can sing again!*

Isaiah says that the earth needs rest and quiet before it can sing, and be at its best. The same is true for each of us. We need times of rest and quiet before we experience the greatest moments of our lives.

Giving birth is one of those great moments. You will expend massive amounts of energy, feel a myriad of emotions, and at the end of it all, you will be holding a beautiful baby. Truly a time to sing. Which means now is the time for quiet and rest.

If this is your first child you are possibly still working full time, and life is hectic preparing for leave. Or this may be child number four, and quiet is non-existent. Either way, the earth requires rest, and so do you. Do what you can to get a good night's sleep. Clear your schedule on the weekends so you can take time to be quiet and refresh yourself.

Life is about to sing, so use the next few weeks to find some quiet and rest.

Confession and prayer: Father, thank You for reminding me to have quiet and rest before my child is born.

Week 22: Day 7

Romans 11:36 (NLT) *For everything comes from him and exists by his power and is intended for his glory. All glory to him forever! Amen.*

Your baby comes from God and exists by His power. What a tremendous thought. Baby has been Heaven sent. God chose your baby to be born in your family at this time. She is the perfect gift from the Lord.

Your child exists by God's power. It is not your body or will that caused baby to exist. She came to be by God's power, and that power continues to sustain her. Nothing that exists by His power is deformed or sick. His power is all she needs to grow into the beautiful little person God intends.

Your child's destiny is to bring glory to God. That is her ultimate purpose. She was conceived, and will be born, to glorify Him.

God, thank You for my baby. Thank You for giving her to us. Thank You that she exists, and is sustained by Your power. I know that Your power makes her fit and perfect in every way. I see my baby bringing glory to You all her life.

Confession and prayer: God, I give You glory for my baby forever and ever. Amen.

Week 23: Day 1

Job 42:15 (NIV) *Nowhere in all the land were there found women as beautiful as Job's daughters, and their father granted them an inheritance along with their brothers.*

With today's technology it is possible for many couples to find out the gender of their child in advance. It can be convenient and exciting to know whether they are a girl or boy, before baby is born.

For whatever reason, some parents are disappointed by their child's gender. Their baby's sex is not what they wanted or expected. In the time of Job, girls weren't the gender you wanted either. Girls could not work as boys do, and eventually they would join another family through marriage. Typically girls were not given an inheritance, but Job did. He did not see his girls any differently to the boys. He loved and cherished them equally.

God has a spiritual inheritance He wants you to give your children, whatever the gender. Mother, you can leave just as great an inheritance for your sons as your daughters. You have something unique and special to install in all your children. Whether your child is a boy or girl, they will be beautiful, and deserve a great spiritual inheritance from you.

Confession and prayer: Lord, I decide to leave a great spiritual inheritance for my beautiful baby boy or girl.

Week 23: Day 2

Isaiah 32:18 (NIV) *My people will live in peaceful dwelling places,*
in secure homes,
in undisturbed places of rest.

One of our basic needs as human beings is that of security. Everyone needs to feel safe. It is wonderful to recognise that God promises to meet that need.

Carrying a child in your body, and being a parent changes the way you do life. Where before you may have taken risks, and perhaps even indulged in adrenaline inducing activities, things are different. Safety is a concern for you and your family.

God promises peaceful dwellings to His people. Homes absent of conflict, division, and anger. He promises tranquillity. The Lord also promises secure homes. Houses safe from thieves, and those who may want to cause harm. Good neighbourhoods and excellent neighbours are a promise from the Lord. And finally, when your home is peaceful and secure, then you will experience undisturbed rest.

God cares about your home life and your home. If you desire a better living situation, take your request to Him. He will give you a peaceful and secure place that will be home sweet home.

Confession and prayer: Father, thank You for caring about my home. I believe that my home will be peaceful, safe, and restful.

Hebrews 13:6 (NLT) *So we can say with confidence, "The Lord is my helper, so I will have no fear. What can mere people do to me?"*

God is your helper today. Go ahead, say it aloud, "The Lord is my helper." He is your helper at work. He is your helper with the kids. He is your helper in every situation.

People have good intentions. Sometimes the best of intentions can cause hurt. They can even bring fear and confusion. First and foremost, the Lord is your helper. Consult Him before making decisions. He wants to help you, be your strength, and give you favour.

Others may say that they have your best interests at heart, but the Lord does. He knows the end from the beginning, and He will help to bring His will to pass. Let the Lord be your helper. Forget about what others may do or say. People may be trying to add support, but with God on your side, His is all the help you need. Humble yourself and receive His help.

Confession and prayer: God, You are my helper. What others do or say is of no concern to me.

Week 23: Day 4

Hebrews 7:10 (NLT) *For although Levi wasn't born yet, the seed from which he came was in Abraham's body when Melchizedek collected the tithe from him.*

Your baby has purpose. As He saw Levi in Abraham's loins, so He saw your child generations ago. God saw and destined her to be born at this time and place. God even knows the children, and grandchildren your child will have. He has an amazing plan for your child built on the greatness of generations who have gone before.

Levi is Abraham's great-grandson. Unfortunately, Abraham never lived to meet Levi on earth. Levi's family line eventually became priests of the Most High. Abraham's actions were sowing a seed for generations to come.

Like it or not, we build upon those who have gone before, and your child will reap from seeds sown long ago. Whether the seeds sown in your family's past were good or bad, allow them to sow good seed into your baby now. Consider having your child dedicated or christened. At the event, allow parents and grandparents to speak good things over your child. Allow the generations to sow life into your little one.

Confession and prayer: Lord, thank You for loving parents and grandparents. We sow good seed for my child's future.

2 Corinthians 4:13 (NLT) *But we continue to preach because we have the same kind of faith the psalmist had when he said, "I believed in God, so I spoke."*

Words are powerful. Words change lives. 2 Corinthians tells us that as a believer you can speak the desired outcome you want in situations, and then see it manifest.

Let's apply that to pregnancy and birth. What is your desired outcome? A healthy child? No complications? No pain? I recommend you be specific and write them down. Express what you have faith for, and what is most important to you. Then start believing and speaking the desired outcome into being.

Speaking what you want is not a magic wand. It is not a guarantee that everything on your list will be granted by your fairy godmother. God is greater and better than that. He longs to give you the desires of your heart because He loves you like no other. Be bold. Speak what you long for regarding birth and pregnancy. Back it up with Scripture, and watch your physical body get in line with what your spirit is saying.

Confession and prayer: I believe, and therefore speak, the desired outcome for my baby, pregnancy, and birth.

Week 23: Day 6

Psalm 33:21 (NLT) *In him our hearts rejoice, for we trust in his holy name.*

It is good for your heart to rejoice. God has been good to you. You're going to have a baby. You're having a wonderful pregnancy. Life is fabulous, be merry!

But what if that isn't your story? Things aren't going well in your pregnancy, and circumstances are stressful? Then, all the more reason to rejoice. 2 Chronicles 20 tells the story of Judah going to fight against the army of Edom. Edom's soldiers were powerful, and defeat looked certain. King Jehoshaphat enquired of the Lord, and God showed him the battle plan - rejoice. The king sent singers ahead of the army to celebrate and praise the Lord. That day, the army of Judah did not even fight, and the enemy was defeated.

So if life is going ahead as planned, rejoice. If you are in the greatest battle you have ever faced, rejoice. Victory is at hand. The Lord will fight for you. Trust in His holy name.

Confession and prayer: Despite my situation, I choose to rejoice in the Lord, today.

Proverbs 22:6 (NLT) *Direct your children onto the right path, and when they are older, they will not leave it.*

You are about to take on the mammoth responsibility of directing your child onto the right path. If you are a first time parent this may seem daunting. But even if you already have children, the way you directed one onto the right path will not be the way that you direct another. Every child is different. Get ready for the ride of your life!

Newborn babies are so precious. They know nothing, and start learning and taking direction from you the first instant they exit the womb. Like sponges, they absorb every moment, form habits, and take cues from your behaviour.

Parenting is not hit and miss. The Bible does not say that if you direct your child on the right path, they might keep following it, but they might not. You may know of good Christian people who raised their children in a godly way, yet now those children are not on the right path. That may be so, but it does not mean the Bible is wrong. Choose to direct your child to live according to the Word of God. You will have to make tough decisions, and at times look like a kill-joy. But you can be guaranteed that when they are older, they will be walking with God. It is a promise from Him.

Confession and prayer: Father, help me direct my children on Your path. My desire is that they will always follow You.

Week 24: Day 1

Psalm 56:4 (NLT) *I praise God for what he has promised. I trust in God, so why should I be afraid? What can mere mortals do to me?*

Many today live in fear of man. They worry about what other people think of them, and desperately want everyone to like them. People think it strange if you don't worry about what others think about you.

How do you live free from being concerned about what other people think? You become concerned with what God thinks. He is thinking about how great you are, and He is excited by the promises He has made to you. He can't wait to see the potential He birthed in you, come to fruition. Your life is exciting, and one big adventure as far as God is concerned.

The psalmist had this kind of revelation. He praised God for His promises. He didn't just praise when the promise came to pass. He praised God when they were just promises. Through praising, he became confident in the Lord, and refused to worry about mere mortals. Revel in the promises He has given you about your baby. It will give you inner confidence, and peace in your magnificent God.

Confession and prayer: Father, I choose to praise You for the promises You have given me about my baby. I praise You before they come to pass, confident that You will do what You have promised.

Week 24: Day 2

Psalm 68:4 (NLT) *Sing praises to God and to his name! Sing loud praises to him who rides the clouds. His name is the Lord— rejoice in his presence!*

My mother has the worst singing voice on the planet. No, she does. We joke about it often. She won't mind that I'm telling you. Does it stop her from singing praises to God? No, no, emphatically no. She loves to sing praise to God, and worship Him as loudly as possible.

I can guarantee you that your voice is not as bad as my mother's. Trust me on this, I can. If she loves to sing praise to God loudly, what is your excuse? No matter how bad we sound to others, praise is a sweet offering to Him. He loves our worship.

Do as the psalmist says and praise the Lord. Sing to His name, rejoice in His presence. He is great and worthy of our praise, because He is God. After all, every mother has to do something that makes her child cringe. Yours might be loudly singing praise to God, er...slightly off key.

Confession and prayer: God, I praise Your name. You ride the clouds. I rejoice in being with You.

Week 24: Day 3

Revelation 1:17 (NLT) *When I saw him, I fell at his feet as if I were dead. But he laid his right hand on me and said, "Don't be afraid! I am the First and the Last.*

Jesus Christ, the Alpha and Omega, the First and the Last. Jesus saw your baby before she was born. He was there at her inception. He knows what she will be like as a teenager, adult, and senior citizen. He knows her first and last, and He holds her in the shadow of His wings.

Jesus Christ is also the first and last word on anything. Whatever the diagnosis or prognosis, that is not the last word. Jesus is the last word. The name of Jesus has the final say. Jesus Christ is the ultimate authority.

Do not be intimidated by what others say. They may lay claim to what goes on in the middle, but Jesus Christ is the First and Last. When all is said and done, the last word is Jesus. Put your trust in Him. Rest in the assurance that the end result will be Jesus Christ, First and Last.

Confession and prayer: I put my hope in You, Jesus Christ, my First and Last.

Week 24: Day 4

James 1:3 (NLT) *For you know that when your faith is tested, your endurance has a chance to grow.*

In a world of instant messaging and fast food, we know little about endurance, and much about the immediate. Human pregnancy is a journey of endurance. If your baby were born the minute she was conceived, she would not survive. Some things are worth waiting for, and require stamina to see them through.

Parenting is a journey of endurance. Teething requires endurance. Toilet training requires endurance, spelling and reading require endurance, and negotiating teenagers requires endurance. Enjoy the moments, laugh through them if you can, and know that all the while you are developing endurance, and an amazing human being.

Pregnancy is the beginning of your child testing you. Use this time to develop tenacity. It will come in handy when the sleepless nights kick in!

Confession and prayer: Lord, develop endurance in me.

Week 24: Day 5

Psalm 68:5 (NLT) *Father to the fatherless, defender of widows—this is God, whose dwelling is holy.*

Celebrating and enjoying pregnancy and parenthood with your husband is lovely. But if you, for whatever reason, are doing it alone, this verse should hold a special place in your heart. Almighty God is Father to the fatherless, defender of widows, and single mothers.

Your baby is not growing up without a father, and you are not doing parenthood alone. You have a partner who has infinite wisdom. He will give you the strength to be a wonderful mother. When you feel lonely, He will always be with you. God will defend you to those who think that you shouldn't be raising children on your own. He cares for you, and doesn't like it when your feelings are hurt.

The Lord will be Father to your children. He will love them, guide them, and make sure they never feel abandoned or deserted. He will lead them, and correct their behaviour, in love and grace. Father will make sure there is enough money to feed and clothe them. They will not go without.

Get to know your child's Father a little more today.

Confession and prayer: Father, thank You for loving and providing for my child. I will not feel alone, but trust You to be my partner in raising children.

Week 24: Day 6

Psalm 104:34 (NLT) *May all my thoughts be pleasing to him, for I rejoice in the Lord.*

Jesus loves you with unconditional love. The Bible says that nothing can separate us from His love. That means no sin can separate a believer from the love of the Father. We can however, do things and think thoughts that do not bring Him pleasure. We assume the types of thoughts that displease God are things like lust, anger, or hatred. But there are other types of thoughts, that you may think every day, that don't please Him.

What thoughts are you considering related to pregnancy and baby? Do you doubt that your child will be healthy and strong? Are you worried about what will happen when you give birth? Thoughts of doubt and anxiety do not please God. The Word tells us to put our trust in Him, and cast our cares on Him.

Determine in yourself that you will cast your worries and cares on the Lord. Think thoughts that are pleasing to Him, such as thoughts of a healthy baby, and happy mamma (you). And don't forget, nothing will separate you from His love.

Confession and prayer: God, I pray that my thoughts today will be pleasing to You.

Week 24: Day 7

Isaiah 65:23 (CEV) *Their work won't be wasted, and their children won't die*
of dreadful diseases. I will bless their children and their grandchildren.

If you read Isaiah 65 in other translations you will find that it says things a little differently. But I want to highlight the way the translators of the Contemporary English Version interpreted this verse. They translated the original Hebrew as, "...and their children won't die of dreadful diseases." The translators cited this portion saying that it is one possible meaning for the difficult Hebrew text.

To me, this is a wonderful translation. There are many dreadful diseases in our world today. It breaks my heart to see horrendous afflictions come upon beautiful children. I have known children who have had to fight grievous illness to survive. Disease should not be part of a child's world. This verse is a promise I claim for my children and family. I do not want them to suffer from any kind of infirmity. The Blood of Jesus protects my family from dreadful diseases.

God does not put ailment on anyone, let alone children. He blesses your children and grandchildren with protection, so that they will not die of dreadful diseases. Stand in faith, and believe this promise for your family.

Confession and prayer: Father, I believe that my children are protected and saved from dying of dreadful diseases, because of the power of the Blood of Jesus.

Week 25: Day 1

Isaiah 49:5 (NLT) *And now the Lord speaks— the one who formed me in my mother's womb to be his servant, who commissioned me to bring Israel back to him.*
The Lord has honored me, and my God has given me strength.

As your child grows you will begin to talk her about her Maker. She will gradually develop an understanding of who God is. In this discovery, she will find that she, and everyone, is created to serve God. That is the purpose of all humankind. We have been crafted as His servants.

Your child has been created with intention. She is born for a reason. Her destiny is to serve God with her whole life, for all her life. Your baby is commissioned with the job of bringing the world back to Jesus. Such an honour!

Baby, you have been created by Most High God. He designed for you to serve Him all your days. God has appointed you to reconcile the world to Jesus. My child, it is an honour to serve the King of kings, and Lord of lords, with all your heart, soul, and strength. Praise God!

Confession and prayer: Father, what an amazing commission for my child. I declare she will serve You.

Week 25: Day 2

Micah 7:7 (NLT) *As for me, I look to the Lord for help. I wait confidently for God to save me, and my God will certainly hear me.*

At times it can feel as through the world does not believe in God. If you are standing for what the Bible says, you may feel like the minority. The prophet Micah was in a similar situation. The people of Israel and Judah were more interested in relying on their own might and intelligence for help. That didn't bother Micah. He looked to the Lord, and waited on Him for an answer.

Today, it may seem that everyone around you is putting their trust in anything but God. You may even feel ridiculed for your stance. Never the less, have an "As for me" attitude. As for me, I look to the Lord. As for me, I wait confidently for Him. As for me, I know He answers prayer. As for me, I look to the Lord to heal my baby.

Jesus is real, His Word is true. As for me, I choose the Lord.

Confession and prayer: I am not swayed by the world. As for me, I look to the Lord.

Week 25: Day 3

Isaiah 49:15 (NLT) *Never! Can a mother forget her nursing child? Can she feel no love for the child she has borne? But even if that were possible, I would not forget you!*

As a woman pregnant with a growing child, Isaiah 49:15 probably horrifies you. You have developed a strong bond, and deep love for your baby. It seems unfathomable that a woman could not love her baby. How could any mother forget, and not love the child she has carried for nine months?

Sadly, it does happen. But God is not like that. Father God does not forget or stop loving His child. In fact, the next verse goes on to say, "See, I have written your name on the palms of my hands." The Hebrew should be translated to read, "Your name has been chiselled on my hand with a nail." Ah, what a picture!

The love a mother has for her children is one of the greatest loves on earth. Even stronger is the love of God. He will never forget His children, or stop loving them. Their names were chiselled into His hand when He hung on the cross. He will never forget you or stop loving you. His love is stronger than the strongest human love. His love is ever reaching for you.

Confession and prayer: Father, thank You for Your overwhelming love.

Psalm 131:2 (CEV) *But I have learned to feel safe and satisfied, just like a young child on its mother's lap.*

One of the delights you will soon experience is getting to know the facial expressions of your little one. The faces she will pull at various times will make you laugh. Cherish those moments. One such face is the smile of a contented baby with a belly full of milk. It is truly precious. Her mouth will make a little smile, (it might be wind, but it is nicer to think of it as a smile) and her body will be fully relaxed. She is safe and satisfied on her mother's lap.

Whenever your child assumes this pose, I pray you remember Psalm 131:2. As you delight in your child's relaxation, and satisfaction now that she is full of all the good stuff, your Heavenly Father delights to see you in this same state. God wants you to climb up on His lap and drink your fill, and once full, rest there, satisfied. He has lots of good things for your life's pleasure. Learn to spend time drinking in His goodness and being satisfied.

Confession and prayer: Father, I climb onto Your lap and drink in Your greatness and glory. I am full and at rest, satisfied in You.

Week 25: Day 5

Judges 13:24 (NLT) *When her son was born, she named him Samson. And the Lord blessed him as he grew up.*

The birth and life of The Biblical character Samson, was miraculous. His parents were originally barren, but after a visitation from an angel of God, Samson's mother became pregnant. The angel promised that Samson would be a man who would carry the Lord's anointing. The Bible tells us that the Lord blessed Samson as he grew up. I am sure that as Samson advanced in age he had an increased awareness of the blessing of God on his life.

The child you carry may be a little like Samson because you struggled to have children for a long time. Yet the Lord came through, and answered your prayer. The Lord will bless your child as she grows. Like Samson, she will have an increased awareness of God and His blessing, the older she becomes. She will carry the anointing of God, and she will use it to bring salvation and blessing to others. God's heart is to bless your child all her life. It really is that simple.

Confession and prayer: God, I believe that You will continue to bless my child as she grows.

Week 25: Day 6

Genesis 17:17 (CEV) *Abraham bowed with his face to the ground and thought, "I am almost a hundred years old. How can I become a father? And Sarah is ninety. How can she have a child?" So he started laughing.*

There are many couples these days who find it difficult to fall pregnant. Then when they find out they are going to have a baby, they complain about pregnancy, and how terrible they feel. They continue to complain about giving birth, and even worse, the child they so longed to have. As the baby grows, they complain about sleepless nights, bad behaviour, and mourn the loss of life as they knew it.

What a shame! If only they had the attitude of Abraham and Sarah. When they found they were having a baby, they laughed. When their baby was born they laughed. And so they would remember to rejoice and laugh through parenthood, they called their baby "laughter."

Being a parent isn't smooth sailing. There are times the bundle of joy will throw tantrums, and make you a bundle of nerves. You may want to complain, yell, and scream, but laugh instead. Being a parent is a gift of gladness. Don't allow anything to rob you of your joy. Abraham was one hundred, and managed to laugh. You can too.

Confession and prayer: Lord, help me not become frustrated and angry as a parent. Let me count everything joy.

Week 25: Day 7

Isaiah 54:14 (NKJV) *In righteousness you shall be established; You shall be far from oppression, for you shall not fear; And from terror, for it shall not come near you.*

When you think of an established garden, you picture mature, healthy trees with beautiful flowers. The plants aren't flimsy or small, but strong and flourishing. The picture of your life is the same when you are established in righteousness. You are strong and healthy. When storms come, you may be shaken, but not uprooted.

The world can be a terrifying place, and things become even more so when you have children that you would die for. When they are away from your side, fear and worry can fill your thoughts, wondering whether some kind of terror may find them. God promises that terror will not come near you or your family when you are established in righteousness.

You can be confident that your children will always return to you unharmed. Establish yourself in righteousness, not your own righteousness, but the righteousness of God. You have been made righteous by the Blood of Jesus. Have no fear, terror will not come near you.

Confession and prayer: I am established in righteousness. I am not worried or fearful of terror.

Week 26: Day 1

Psalm 127:4 (NLT) *Children born to a young man are like arrows in a warrior's hands.*

Archery and the use of a bow and arrow is not common in our society. When you think about it, arrows are sticks. Sticks that have been shaped and formed with purpose. When aimed, they produce deadly results.

You can approach parenthood in a haphazard kind of way, hoping that your children turn out alright. Or you can treat them like arrows. You can train your child with purpose. You can point her in the right direction. You can make sure her life is aimed at fulfilling her destiny. You can see her as a mighty weapon that will have deadly results against the kingdom of darkness on this earth.

Even at a young age, your child is an arrow. She is a weapon of mass destruction not just in the toy room (or any room of the house for that matter), but for the kingdom. Train and aim her well. With great power comes great responsibility.

Confession and prayer: God, I will train my child and aim her towards her destiny. She will be a mighty weapon against the devil.

Week 26: Day 2

Ecclesiastes 11:5 (NLT) *Just as you cannot understand the path of the wind or the mystery of a tiny baby growing in its mother's womb, so you cannot understand the activity of God, who does all things.*

The baby growing in your womb is a wonderful mystery. While you may be able to see glimpses of your child in scans and various types of imaging, what she looks like, her personality, and heart are but a mystery until her birth.

As amazing as medical science is, Ecclesiastes tells us we will never fully understand how a baby grows in her mother's womb. What shapes her personality and temperament before she is born? What determines whether she looks like mum or dad the most? God understands. He more than knows how your baby is growing, He orchestrates it. He is in complete control of the process.

People are often afraid of what they don't understand. In this case you don't have to be. Don't be fearful of whether your child is growing correctly. God knows how your child is progressing. He is giving her a beautiful personality and smile. He made the wind, your baby, and He does all things. Put your trust in Him.

Confession and prayer: God, I don't understand how You are making my baby, but I know that You are in control.

Week 26: Day 3

Proverbs 3:12 (NLT) *For the Lord corrects those he loves, just as a father corrects a child in whom he delights.*

Correcting and disciplining your child is part of parenthood. Discipline, especially when it comes to smacking a child, is a highly debated topic. There are a few thoughts you may want to consider when it comes time to correct your child.

Proverbs says the Lord corrects those He loves. All correction and discipline needs to stem from love, not anger or frustration. Your little one may have disobeyed, but most of the time she delights you. Remember that.

When the Lord corrects you, He does so gently, and with grace. He quickly forgives. He also corrects in a manner that suits your personally and temperament, so that you respond well. You might consider doing the same with your children. Get to know what each child will respond to, and work with her accordingly. Take your Heavenly Father's lead, and correct your children in grace and love.

Confession and prayer: I will never correct my child out of anger. I will correct her in love.

Week 26: Day 4

Luke 1:30 (NLT) *"Don't be afraid, Mary," the angel told her, "for you have found favor with God!"*

In a world that doesn't seem to do anyone any favours, it is comforting to know that you have found favour with God. He speaks the same words to you as He did to Mary millennia ago, "Don't be afraid, you have found favour with me."

Mary certainly didn't find favour with man by falling pregnant. Her condition was most likely the town gossip, and her family ostracised. Friends perhaps turned into enemies, and she was treated with contempt. Such things did not bother Mary, she was favoured of God.

As you enter the last few months of pregnancy, don't be afraid. God is looking after you. His favour is on you. And when His favour is on you, it is all you need. Pay no attention to how you are being treated. Don't let little things get you down. You are favoured of the Lord, and that's what counts.

Confession and prayer: God, I focus on your favour rather than the favour of man.

Week 26: Day 5

1 Peter 3:12 (NKJV) *For the eyes of the Lord are on the righteous, And His ears are open to their prayers; But the face of the Lord is against those who do evil.*

Babies born at 26 weeks gestation survive. They have to fight, but they survive, and eventually thrive. God's hand of grace and healing is on such children. He has a purpose for every soul, and wants every child to live.

If premature babies are in your family history, or if your doctor has fears that you will give birth prematurely, know that God is a God of miracles. His eyes are on the righteous (which is you according to 2 Corinthians 5:21). He hears your prayers. If your baby has not been born, let your prayer be that she arrives full term. It is certainly a less traumatic start to life. But if she is born prematurely, pray for a miracle. Pray for improvement every day. Pray that she will develop like a child born at term. Pray that she will not suffer any side effects from medication, or her early arrival.

God has His eyes on you and your baby. She will be born at the perfect time, and He will answer your prayers for her.

Confession and prayer: Father, I pray for all premature babies that are fighting to live. Breathe into them, today.

Week 26: Day 6

Jeremiah 23:4 (NLT) *Then I will appoint responsible shepherds who will care for them, and they will never be afraid again. Not a single one will be lost or missing. I, the Lord, have spoken!*

I am sure that you can think of motion pictures, or real life news headlines, where children were abducted. Such horrific realities can make you fearful. They are anyone's worst nightmare. Jeremiah 23:4 is another verse to pray over your children. God will care for them, and make sure that none will be lost or missing.

One day you and the family will be in a crowded place. In a split second, you will turn around to discover one child is gone. It is tempting to panic. You don't have to be anxious. None will be lost or missing. You will be reunited with your child.

Father God has His eyes on your child ever and always. He will bring your children back to you. He will use good people, and sometimes even angels, but they will always return. None lost or missing. The Lord has spoken. Believe it.

Confession and prayer: Father, I do not fear. My child will never be lost or missing. If she is, You will bring her back.

Week 26: Day 7

Exodus 2:9 (NLT) *"Take this baby and nurse him for me," the princess told the baby's mother. "I will pay you for your help." So the woman took her baby home and nursed him.*

Having a child is expensive. There are medical charges, the cost of clothing and nursery items, nappies, not to mention her education, and providing for her every need for the rest of her life. Children don't come cheap, but you wouldn't have it any other way.

In Exodus, God supernaturally provided finances to raise the child Moses. The family thought that their child would not be provided for, and that he would have to die. Instead, God turned things around, and not only did Moses live, but his tuition, and any expenses involved in raising him, were completely taken care of.

God has financial provision for your baby. You don't need to worry about her schooling, or where money will come from to buy her nappies. As He supernaturally provided for Moses, God will miraculously supply for your baby. God has a plan and purpose for your child,
as He did for the baby Moses. He will turn situations around to provide for her.

Confession and prayer: Thank You, Jesus, for Your supernatural provision for my child.

Week 27: Day 1

Galatians 3:13 (NLT) *But Christ has rescued us from the curse pronounced by the law. When he was hung on the cross, he took upon himself the curse for our wrongdoing. For it is written in the Scriptures, "Cursed is everyone who is hung on a tree."*

Today begins a series of devotions related to your labour and delivery. The Apostle Paul wrote in Galatians that Jesus bore the curse for wrongdoing when He hung on the cross. What does that mean and how does it relate to giving birth?

After Adam and Eve disobeyed God in the Garden of Eden, God pronounced three curses - one for the snake, one for the man, and one for the woman. The curse pronounced over the woman reads:

"I will sharpen the pain of your pregnancy, and in pain you will give birth. And you will desire to control your husband, but he will rule over you." (Genesis 3:16 NLT)

Experiencing pain in childbirth, and labouring to bring forth a child is a curse that was pronounced almost at the beginning of time. The good news is that the curse has been broken because of the Cross of Christ. The even better news is that you don't have to experience pain in childbirth.

Now here's some physiology: pain in childbirth is because the muscles of the uterus begin to fatigue. They don't get used often, so they fatigue easily. But God has made a way for you to have a supernatural childbirth experience. The muscles of your uterine wall don't have to go into fatigue and cause you pain. How will that happen? It will be a miracle, yet it is possible because you have been redeemed of the curse of pain in childbirth.

Childbirth with pain is labour, but without pain it is supernatural.

Confession and prayer: Pain is part of the curse. I confess I will experience no pain in childbirth because Christ rescued me from the curse. My abdominal muscles and uterine muscles will contract without experiencing fatigue.

Week 27: Day 2

Exodus 1:19 (NLT) *"The Hebrew women are not like the Egyptian women," the midwives replied. "They are more vigorous and have their babies so quickly that we cannot get there in time."*

If you have not done so already, I encourage you to get a picture in your mind of the kind of birthing experience you desire. Be as specific as you can. To me, the best kind of birth for you and baby is a fast one.

The longer the labour, the higher the risk of complications for both mother and baby. If the women of Israel had a long birth, death of their male offspring was certain. Having babies quickly was a matter of life and death. God enabled the Hebrew women to give birth fast, and with lots of energy.

If your desire is for a vaginal birth, you will probably also want it to be quick. It may not seem possible, especially if this is your first child, but God made it so for the Hebrew women during the time of Moses. God wants to give you the same birth that they had – fast and vigorous.

Believe God for an active and forceful birth. Believe that your cervix will dilate quickly, and that your child will make her way through the birthing canal with ease. God's desire is a blessed birth for you.

Confession and prayer: I believe I will have my children quickly. My birth will be dynamic and active.

Week 27: Day 3

1 John 4:18 (NLT) *Such love has no fear, because perfect love expels all fear. If we are afraid, it is for fear of punishment, and this shows that we have not fully experienced his perfect love.*

During labour and delivery there are a number of hormones that play important roles. One hormone is adrenaline. Adrenaline is often referred to as the fight or flight hormone. It is activated and released in dangerous situations. It does things like make your senses sharper, and causes muscles to contract faster. It can also paralyse a person in fear, and make systems shut down.

Adrenaline is released in labour. It is released to help your uterine muscles contract faster and work better. It is released in excess. If the excess adrenaline is not used up, the opposite can start to happen. Muscles become paralysed in fear. This is not what you want.

On a practical level, you want to keep your body moving through your contractions as much as possible to use up the adrenaline. On a spiritual level, you can make this confession: This baby was conceived in perfect love so there is no fear in the pregnancy or birth process.

Do not allow fear into the birthing suite. Do not allow adrenaline to overpower you. Your baby was conceived, and continues, to grow in love. Your body will not be paralysed in fear. Perfect, godly love drives out fear.

Confession and prayer: Father, I release love in my body, not fear.

Week 27: Day 4

2 Timothy 1:7 (NKJV) *For God has not given us a spirit of fear, but of power and of love and of a sound mind.*

When you are labouring hard, it is easy for the pain and fear to take over. Your mind starts to panic, and things get out of control. 2 Timothy 1:7 says that God has not given us a spirit of fear but of sound mind. Believe that even as your contractions hit their peak, you continue to have a sound mind.

It is good to have a birthing plan of what you want for labour and delivery, but what you get may be far from that. If things go wrong, you and your husband will be forced to make quick decisions. You will both need a sound mind to make right ones.

Whether issues with your pregnancy, the unknowns of birth, or labour and delivery cause you to fear, remind yourself that is not the spirit you have been given. You have a spirit of power, love, and sound mind. You can think clearly. You can make wise decisions in an instant. You have a composed and sound mind.

Confession and prayer: I will have a calm and sound mind through the birthing process.

Romans 10:17 (NKJV) *So then faith comes by hearing, and hearing by the word of God.*

Hebrews 11:1 says that faith is the substance of things hoped for, and evidence of the unseen. Every labour and birth is different. If this is not your first pregnancy, you can use your previous birthing experience as a guide, but it will not be the same. Your birthing experience is unknown and unseen right now.

If the birth you desire is pain-free, quick, and without complications, it is by faith. You can think nice thoughts about your labour and delivery, but that will do nothing except make you feel good. Feeling good is nice, but if you want to receive what you believe, then faith has to come through the Word of God.

The way faith comes through the Word of God is quite simple. You apply Scripture to your situation. Hopefully, this devotion has taught you what that looks like, and you have been doing it for some time. The past three devotions are perfect examples.

When you apply the Bible to your situation, your words are not empty. They are evidence that what you are saying will come to pass. Faith comes through the Word.

Confession and prayer: I have faith in a wonderful birth because faith has come through hearing and confessing the Word of God.

Week 27: Day 6

Philippians 1:6 (NLT) *And I am certain that God, who began the good work within you, will continue his work until it is finally finished on the day when Christ Jesus returns.*

Some twenty-seven weeks ago, God began the good work of creating a baby in you. And God will certainly continue that good work until He is finished, and baby is ready to be born. Not only will she be fully grown, and ready to tackle the world, but she will be in the correct position for birth.

If you have a history of breach babies, speak this verse over your child. Tell her that God will finish the good work He started by causing her to be in the right position. Babies can turn in the womb even very late. Of course you want her facing downwards as early as possible, but don't let your child's position worry you. God will finish the work, and that means getting her ready to pass through the birth canal.

God never leaves anything unfinished. He will complete the good work He has started.

Confession and prayer: God began the good work of baby growing within me. He will continue it until baby is fully grown, and in the correct position in the womb for birth.

Week 27: Day 7

Philippians 4:19 (NLT) *And this same God who takes care of me will supply all your needs from his glorious riches, which have been given to us in Christ Jesus.*

God is rich in love, care, and goodness for you and me. He has abundant supply of whatever we need. He will meet your needs through the provision of the Blood of Jesus.

Your needs are not just financial or material. If you have needs and desires for your birth, God wants to meet them. Not some of them, all of them. He will supply.

So the next question is, what are your needs for baby's birth? Have you thought about what you want? Be specific. Tell God that you don't want an epidural. Tell Him that you want your labour to commence naturally. Or if you are having a caesarean delivery, tell God that you want a speedy recovery, and a small scar. Give Him all the details. Once you have, begin confessing, and believing that He will supply those needs.

Father God loves to supply your need.

Confession and prayer: I will have the birth I desire because God supplies all my needs.

Week 28: Day 1

James 3:2 (NLT) *Indeed, we all make many mistakes. For if we could control our tongues, we would be perfect and could also control ourselves in every other way.*

What is the most powerful muscle in your body? Your quads? Maybe your pecks? Oh, wait, your heart? No, the most powerful muscle in your body belongs to your tongue. That's what the Bible says, and God is always right.

"If we could control our tongues, we...could control ourselves in every way."

Your tongue can control everything about you - health, career, emotions, and thoughts. If your tongue says it, your body will get in line. Your tongue has ultimate control.

Let's apply this to giving birth. Your tongue can tell your body how to bring your baby into the world. Whatever you say with your mouth controls your whole body, so whatever you speak about baby's birth will happen in your body.

This is a confession I wrote for my tongue to speak over my body: *With my words I stay in control of my birth. I tell my body to create endorphins (to block pain). I tell my body to create oxytocins (to increase the efficiency of contractions). I utilise adrenaline with action, but do not let it take over. The baby will press down on my uterus more and more with each contraction. Uterine muscles, you will not fatigue. Cervix, open to ten centimetres. Perineum, stretch gently so that baby can pass through without tearing.*

Use the tongue to speak to your body, and to speak the Word of God.

Confession and prayer: My body will do what I speak because I speak the Word of God.

Week 28: Day 2

Romans 8:37 (NLT) *No, despite all these things, overwhelming victory is ours through Christ, who loved us.*

The last verse to confess related to giving birth is this: overwhelming victory is mine. Whether you have a great labour and birth, or whether things deviate from the plan, in the end you will be holding a beautiful, healthy child. Yes, overwhelming victory is yours. Life has triumphed.

All the hard work is done. Now it's time to celebrate the miracle of life. A baby has been born. A ray of sunshine has come into the world. Life will never be the same.

Your child is a victory. Couples often say that children are the best thing they have ever done. It is true. Children are a great gift.

Whatever happens in the lead up to her birth, when it is all said and done, you will hold one of your greatest triumphs. Treasure her. Love her and celebrate her. You hold in your arms a trophy of God's favour and goodness.

Confession and prayer: In all this, I have overwhelming victory.

Week 28: Day 3

Romans 8:1 (NLT) *So now there is no condemnation for those who belong to Christ Jesus.*

I wish I could tell you that after confessing Scripture and building faith, I had two pain-free deliveries where everything went according to plan. I didn't. My first pregnancy was a blighted ovum and ended in miscarriage. My oldest son was induced, and then born by emergency caesarean. My second son was born naturally, but I still needed an epidural and stitches. So what about the last week of devotions?

My experience does not make the Word of God wrong. I prayed and believed but it didn't happen. It is not because God is angry or punishing me. I didn't have unconfessed sin in my life that was blocking my miracle. There is no condemnation for those who are in Christ.

My prayer is that through this devotion, many many women believe the Word, and receive pain-free amazing births. The Bible says we are redeemed from the curse, and I believe it. Even though I did not experience it myself, I know God wants to do it for others.

But if your experience is like mine, where you believe, but don't quite receive, remember you did not fail. God did not fail. Give all that happened to God, and know that there is no condemnation.

Confession and prayer: Father, I thank You that You will never condemn me or make me feel guilty.

Week 28: Day 4

Psalm 37:25 (NLT) *Once I was young, and now I am old. Yet I have never seen the godly abandoned or their children begging for bread.*

It is hard to imagine what life will be like when you are one hundred years old. Anyone alive now who is that age, has seen the world go through incredible changes. Though the world may change, the Word of God stays the same. And what was true centuries ago, remains true today.

God provides for the children of the godly. He was doing it while you were young, and He will continue to do so when you are old. God will provide for your children. They will not go begging for bread, clothing, or anything they need. Education, their first car, music lessons, and sports equipment, God will not leave your children begging.

Don't let the worry of providing for your children hinder you. Don't let it stop you from having more children. God provides for the children of the godly. He has done so for millennia, and will continue until Christ's return.

Confession and prayer: Thank You, God, that You supply for the needs of my children.

Week 28: Day 5

Isaiah 66:13 (NLT) *I will comfort you there in Jerusalem as a mother comforts her child.*

When your baby is in some kind of pain, nothing beats being comforted by mum. There may be other willing hands reaching out to console a child, but she will not be satisfied until she is in the arms of her mother. When your baby searches you out like that, it melts your heart. You will hug and kiss her, and hold her tight until everything is better.

That is the heart of a mother, and any loving parent would respond in such a way. Your heart breaks when you hear your baby's cry.

Father God in Heaven loves you, and will comfort you when you reach for Him. If loving parents treat their children in such a way, how much more will God of creation comfort His children? He is a good God. He does not like to see us hurting. He comforts the grieving. He is not pointing a finger in judgement, instead God reaches in love. Receive His comfort.

Confession and prayer: God, I receive Your comfort, love, and forgiveness.

Week 28: Day 6

Matthew 21:21 (NLT) *Then Jesus told them, "I tell you the truth, if you have faith and don't doubt, you can do things like this and much more. You can even say to this mountain, 'May you be lifted up and thrown into the sea,' and it will happen."*

Mountain moving faith is what Jesus talked about and demonstrated. He walked on water. He spoke peace to raging storms. He healed incurable diseases. He cast out demonic spirits. He raised the dead. And He did all this as a man because He had faith in God.

Jesus said that you and I can do even greater things than He did. If you believe and don't doubt, you will have mountain moving faith. You can speak to the mountain, or whatever situation you face, and it will move.

A few days ago we spoke about pain-free labour and birth. It may seem like an impossible mountain, but if you believe and don't doubt, you can speak to that situation, and see God work a miracle. Your mountain may be delivering a healthy and whole baby, when you have been told the likelihood is small. Whatever it is, speak to it in Jesus name, and tell it to move. Mountain moving faith is your destiny.

Confession and prayer: God, I believe and don't doubt. I speak to the mountain I face, and see it move in Jesus name.

Week 28: Day 7

1 Timothy 5:10 (NLT) *She must be well respected by everyone because of the good she has done. Has she brought up her children well? Has she been kind to strangers and served other believers humbly? Has she helped those who are in trouble? Has she always been ready to do good?*

In context, 1 Timothy 5:10 is talking about widows over sixty years of age. There wouldn't be too many sixty year old widows having babies, I suspect. So why this Scripture? Because it is talking about the kind of woman she was as a younger person.

This is the kind of woman God wants you and I to be. He wants you to do good, and win the respect of others. He wants you to bring up your children well. Children who are honourable and successful, hard working and disciplined. A woman who is humble and kind to people she does not know, even when no one is watching. God is looking for a woman who helps the troubled - a neighbour, a child's friend. And finally, God looks for someone with an eye for opportunities to do good.

Don't try to be a cool or trendy mum. The kind of woman described here is the type of mother your children need. Ladies, that is what we should aspire to.

Confession and prayer: Lord, I want to be a godly mother.

Week 29: Day 1

Hebrews 12:1 (NLT) *Therefore, since we are surrounded by such a huge crowd of witnesses to the life of faith, let us strip off every weight that slows us down, especially the sin that so easily trips us up. And let us run with endurance the race God has set before us.*

Pregnancy may seem to be an endurance event, like a marathon or triathlon. In reality, it is quite small. Being a parent is the real endurance race. It will prove to be one of life's most challenging experiences. Nothing compares to it. Parenthood will throw curve ball after curve ball. Be strong and endure.

Hebrews tells us that in the race of life we are surrounded by a great cloud of witnesses. While the author is referring to fathers and mothers in the faith who have gone before and have now passed, that crowd can also include loved ones in your life, such as your own parents, grandparents, uncles, aunts, and dear friends. When things are challenging as a parent, you are not alone. Draw on the strength of the crowd around you. They will not judge you. God has placed them in your life to cheer you on.

The other advice given is to strip off every weight that slows you down. When children start to stress you out, strip off the unimportant things that can wait. Leave the washing, cleaning, and other non-essentials until a time when you are feeling better.

Keep running the race of being wonder-parent, super-mum, and career-woman. Be encouraged by those around you, don't be afraid to ask for help, and skip the non-essentials. You're a winner.

Confession and prayer: Father, help me run the race of parenthood well.

Week 29: Day 2

Proverbs 31:10 (NLT) *Who can find a virtuous and capable wife? She is more precious than rubies.*

Today, we begin a series of devotions based on the godly woman of Proverbs 31. Some don't believe that it is possible for one woman to be the Proverbs 31 woman, but I beg to differ. It is possible. She does exist. She could even be you! We focus on certain Scriptures from Proverbs 31 that I believe pertain especially to motherhood.

Verse ten is a reminder: Woman, you are precious, more precious than rubies. You are worthy of love, rest, respect, and care.

Sometimes being a mother means forgoing your needs for the benefit of the family. While that is part of being a mother, the old saying still stands, "Happy wife, happy life." When mum is healthy and thriving, the rest of the family will also.

You are special. Treat yourself with respect. Keep your body healthy. Sacrifice for your family but don't become a martyr. Value yourself. You are precious.

Confession and prayer: Father God, I value myself and recognise that I am precious in Your eyes.

Week 29: Day 3

Proverbs 31:15 (NLT) *She gets up before dawn to prepare breakfast for her household and plan the day's work for her servant girls.*

If this is your first child then I have news for you: sleep-ins are over. That's right, children, especially babies, are early risers, hence you will be also. Getting up before dawn will be a regular occurrence with a baby in your life. The world is an exciting place for her to explore. She certainly does not want to stay asleep when the sun is up, even if it is only slightly up!

Being forced to wake early can be a good thing. Life can be highly productive early in the morning. You can achieve a lot before midday. It is the attitude of the Proverbs 31 mother. She wakes up before everyone else and makes plans.

You may not be a person who likes structure, and tend to live on the fly. Babies and children thrive on structure. Making plans and having a routine helps babies and toddlers sleep, eat, and play better.

So if mornings aren't your thing, they will be, and for good reason. Plan the day for you and baby. Get into a predictable routine. It will make life with a little person a whole lot easier.

Confession and prayer: Father, help me set a realistic routine, and cope with early mornings!

Week 29: Day 4

Proverbs 31:17 (NLT) *She is energetic and strong, a hard worker.*

Being a mother requires energy, strength, and hard work. It begins during pregnancy as your baby becomes heavier, and daily tasks more tiresome. Then there is birth. Giving birth is hard work. It is more intense than any personal training session you will have. It is most likely to be the hardest you will push your body in your life.

That all precedes motherhood. Boy, do you need energy and strength for that. It is wonderful to be a mother, but it is no easy ride. It will take you to the edge and push boundaries. Being a mother is not one dimensional. It requires energy and strength physically, emotionally, mentally, and spiritually. Oh, and there's no clocking off from this job. Of course the Proverbs 31 woman is energetic, strong, and a hard worker. She has to be. It comes with the territory.

In saying all this, mothers must get their energy and strength from somewhere, so look after yourself. Eat well, exercise, avoid stress, and spend time refreshing yourself with Jesus. That is how you will have the energy and strength you need for the monumental task of raising children.

Confession and prayer: Father, I draw my strength and energy from You. Refresh my life today.

Week 29: Day 5

Proverbs 31:18 (NLT) *She makes sure her dealings are profitable; her lamp burns late into the night.*

Not only does motherhood involve early mornings, but often it includes late nights, or waking late into the night. Burning the candle at both ends is the life of a mother with young children.

Make sure that what you do is profitable. Mothers are time poor. There is always more things to do than hours in the day. The key to still getting things done is to prioritise, cut back, and make sure that what you do is profitable.

Spending time with your husband and children is always profitable. There are however, things that a woman may do that are not profitable. If you want to get more out of life, take a good, hard look at things. What relationships are not profitable? What habits are not profitable? Get rid of things that will not bring you joy, peace, love, and fulfilment. Perhaps then your candle won't burn quite so late into the night.

Confession and prayer: Father, I want a profitable life. Draw my attention to unprofitable habits, and help me to change.

Week 29: Day 6

Proverbs 31:25 (NLT) *She is clothed with strength and dignity, and she laughs without fear of the future.*

Watching the six o'clock news will leave anyone fearful of what the future holds. What kind of world will my child grow up in? The Bible does not teach that we should be afraid of the future, in fact it teaches we should laugh about it. Not a sinister laugh that says, "So what if I'm leaving my kids a horrible future," but one that is confident and happy about what is in store.

The world will get worse, Jesus said this two thousand years ago. But for believers, the world will only get better. That does not mean that you can sit back and relax when it comes to raising your child. You will need to be diligent. You will need to guide her friendship and media choices. And you may even need to fight for her very life, physically as well as spiritually - all the while, knowing that God has a wonderful future for your child. You can smile and laugh as you think of the beautiful future He has for the baby in your womb. What lies ahead is delightful.

Confession and prayer: God, I smile, and look forward to the wondrous future You have for my baby.

Proverbs 31:26 (NLT) *When she speaks, her words are wise, and she gives instructions with kindness.*

Give instruction with kindness - boy, have I messed up sometimes when it comes to this. I dare say that there will be at least one occasion when you will mess up too. Yes, your own flesh and blood can be exasperating. So much so, that instruction will not be given with kindness, but with yelling, frustration, and even anger. Praise God for His forgiveness, and for loving and forgiving children.

Proverbs tells us that the ideal woman utters wise words in kindness. That should be every mother's goal. Though we fall short, it is what we aspire to.

So the next time your gorgeous child takes you to the brink of losing it, remember this verse. Be wise, and give your instruction with kindness. Answer the question for the thousandth time. Tell her to stop, again. Ask her to put her toys away, again. You are the Proverbs 31 woman. You speak wisdom in kindness.

Confession and prayer: Lord, help me to give my children instruction with kindness. (Really, really help me!)

Week 30: Day 1

Proverbs 31:28-29 (NLT) *Her children stand and bless her. Her husband praises her:"There are many virtuous and capable women in the world, but you surpass them all!"*

Naturally, women are often their own worst critic. We are well aware of our shortcomings, and oblivious to those of others. It does not take much for a woman to be down on herself. That is why God places a loving husband, and grateful children in a mother's life - to make her blatantly aware of her amazing capabilities. Yes Mum, you do surpass them all!

Media celebrates women who are anything but virtuous. There is a serious lack of goodness in the lives of many women. The Bible on the other hand, says that a noble woman is the one who should be celebrated and praised. She is a hero, a true role model.

Accept praise and adoration from your family, and others. You are an excellent mother and woman. You are upright, and extremely capable. You deserve blessing, and all the cuddles and kisses your children give. There is no one quite like you.

Confession and prayer: I accept blessing and praise for the godly life I lead.

Proverbs 31:30 (NLT) *Charm is deceptive, and beauty does not last; but a woman who fears the Lord will be greatly praised.*

Every mother wants her children to admire her. We want to be seen as a hero in their eyes. Because of this, mothers will do their best to be cool. A mother may attempt to win her child's approval by acting more like a friend. This type of behaviour may seem to promote free communication and an open relationship, but in reality it is wrought with danger.

Your child will have many friends. She does not need more friends, she needs a mother. The Bible says that charm and beauty will not gain your child's affections. The type of mother your baby needs is one who fears the Lord. A mother who daily spends time in His presence. A mother who has found her identity in being a daughter of the King. A woman who does not care about the opinion of others, but instead delights in the opinion of God Almighty. That is the type of woman who will have a long and successful relationship with her children. She will be seen as a hero in their eyes.

Confession and prayer: Father, Your opinion and ways are what matter most to me. I do not focus on how I look, I will be a mother after Your heart.

Week 30: Day 3

Ezekiel 36:30 (NKJV) *And I will multiply the fruit of your trees and the increase of your fields, so that you need never again bear the reproach of famine among the nations.*

Famine is horrific. The worst part about famine is that those affected by it most are children. Children are dying because they do not have enough clean water or food. It is a reproach on society that this is still the case.

Our God does not have limited resources at His disposal. He is the God of more than enough. He is the God of increase and multiplication. God wants to increase you, because you will use those resources to help others. He knows He can trust believers because they have His heart.

God is increasing your family. The world will tell you that children are money and resource guzzlers. That is not God's opinion. He sees your baby as a way of multiplying you. He can use your family to bring His kingdom to earth even more, with the addition of your baby. You and your family are God's solution for the world. He is multiplying you so that you will bring change.

Confession and prayer: God, You have a great vision and plan for me and my family. Open our eyes that we may use the resources You have given us wisely.

Week 30: Day 4

Psalm 37:30 (NLT) *The godly offer good counsel; they teach right from wrong.*

It is your job, as a parent, to teach your children what is right. It is not the job of the government, school or even church. It is the role of the parent. When you teach your children right from wrong, they will continue to live a moral life in adulthood. What you teach your child has far greater impact than any government body or significant person in her life.

Lack of strong parenting is one of the biggest problems in the world today. If parents taught their children right from wrong, society would be a better place. The issue is, parents are time poor. When they spend time with their children, they do not want to perform discipline, and be the bad guy. So instead of doing their job, parents let children do as they please.

Children need parents who will teach them right from wrong, not ones who want to be liked. Provide your children with good counsel. Ultimately they will thank you for it.

Confession and prayer: God, I take responsibility for teaching my children right from wrong.

Week 30: Day 5

Luke 1:37 (NLT) *For nothing is impossible with God.*

Whatever you are believing God for today, nothing is impossible to Him. Whether it be a pain-free delivery or an uncomplicated caesarean, God can grant your request. I know we have been here before, but in a world full of doubt and fear, we need constant reminders of God's goodness and miracle-working power. We need encouragement to keep the faith.

Nothing - no thing is impossible to Him. In context, this verse is referring to the virgin birth of Jesus Christ. It is impossible for a virgin to fall pregnant, yet God made it so. Impossible is His speciality. He walks on water, heals all disease, and will accomplish what you desire.

Never stop believing. Never give up hope. God is God of the impossible. Nothing is impossible to Him.

Stand firm, and continue to believe for the type of birth experience you desire, no matter how impossible. Regardless of what others say, put your hope in God. With Him, nothing is impossible.

Confession and prayer: God, I believe that You will do the impossible in my life.

Week 30: Day 6

Proverbs 23:24 (NLT) *The father of godly children has cause for joy. What a pleasure to have children who are wise.*

It is never too early to start praying for your children. I know of many couples who began praying for their children, well before they started trying to fall pregnant. Two of the greatest character traits you could hope for in your children are mentioned in Proverbs 23:24, godliness and wisdom. I don't know about you, but I want my children to be known as godly and wise.

Unfortunately, children are not born with godliness and wisdom. It is something they learn, and you are their greatest teacher. Take every opportunity to teach your children to love God and His ways. Invest in resources that teach worship and values. Talk to them about making good choices, teaching principles of honour and obedience.

But most of all, your children will learn godliness and wisdom by your actions. They are watching your choices and attitudes. They will mimic your life. The best way to guarantee godly and wise children is to be that yourself. It is how godliness and wisdom are birthed in the lives of the young.

Confession and prayer: I want to teach my children to be godly and wise.

Week 30: Day 7

Psalm 52:8 (NLT) *But I am like an olive tree, thriving in the house of God. I will always trust in God's unfailing love.*

Once a child comes into your life, she easily becomes the centre of attention. Life revolves around her, and meeting her needs before anyone else, including yourself. While there is nothing inherently wrong with that, it is important to keep in mind that the best way to look after your child is to thrive in your own life.

You have been created to thrive, not survive. There will be times as a parent that you feel as though you are surviving. Survival is bearable for a short amount of time, but if maintained for longer periods, it can lead to unhappiness.

Psalm 52 tells us that the ultimate way to thrive in life, is in His house. You may have not been to church in a while, or perhaps you have never been. Let me encourage you, God wants your life to thrive, and the best way for that to happen is by going to church. Find a church you enjoy and attend regularly. It's good for you, and it's good for your baby.

Confession and prayer: Father, I choose to thrive in Your house.

Week 31: Day 1

James 5:7 (NLT) *Dear brothers and sisters, be patient as you wait for the Lord's return. Consider the farmers who patiently wait for the rains in the fall and in the spring. They eagerly look for the valuable harvest to ripen.*

How do you feel when you are not in control of what is happening in your life? Does it cause stress and worry? Or are you comfortable and easy going? My guess is that most would be the latter. We live in a world of control, and have become control freaks!

James encourages us to learn from the life of a farmer. Farmers prepare the soil, sow seed, do whatever else needs to be done, and then they wait. They cannot make rain fall. Once their side of the work is done, they let God do His. We should do likewise.

There is not terribly much in the modern world that is out of our control. However, pregnancy and giving birth are some of those things. Write all the birth plans you like, but when the time comes, you may have to have an emergency caesarean.

Be patient, and be prepared to roll with the punches. Do all you know to do, and then leave it to Him. Trust God to send what you need, when the time is right. Your baby will be healthy and strong, whether everything goes to plan, or not. Rest in faith knowing God is in control.

Confession and prayer: Lord, I release control of my child's birth to You.

Week 31: Day 2

Mark 10:13 (NLT) *One day some parents brought their children to Jesus so he could touch and bless them. But the disciples scolded the parents for bothering him.*

Can you imagine that day? Jesus tenderly touching and blessing the children. It must have been so amazing to physically feel the Lord's embrace, to see Him smile and laugh.

You may have heard the saying, "Children should be seen and not heard." It was not taken from the Bible. Jesus always has time for children. They are not forgotten or an afterthought. His arms are open wide to them.

Your children will always be the apple of your eye. Jesus sees them the same. He loves your babies even more than you do.

Be sure to introduce this Jesus to your baby. Tell your child of Jesus' amazing love for her. He will never be too busy, or push her away. He is up for a cuddle whenever she needs. Remind her that the touch and blessing of Jesus is upon her life everywhere she goes.

Confession and prayer: Jesus, thank You for Your touch and blessing upon my baby.

Week 31: Day 3

Deuteronomy 5:16 (NLT) *Honor your father and mother, as the Lord your God commanded you. Then you will live a long, full life in the land the Lord your God is giving you.*

Honour is a word seldom mentioned in today's vernacular. You honour someone in the armed forces, but not anywhere else. Does anyone know what honour is?

Honour is a Bible word. To honour your father and mother carries more weight than to merely respect them. Honouring is what God commands. To honour your parents means to esteem and value them. You place them in high regard. You never speak ill of them, or speak to them in disrespecting tone. Despite what they have or have not done, your father and mother deserve honour.

Honour is not something your child will pick up. The world around her will not teach her how to honour. It is your job as a parent to teach your child to honour you. You are deserving of honour, and have the Biblical right to expect honour. A godly family is one that honours each other.

Confession and prayer: Father, help me to teach my children to honour me, by showing honour to my own parents.

Week 31: Day 4

Zechariah 8:12 (NLT) *For I am planting seeds of peace and prosperity among you. The grapevines will be heavy with fruit. The earth will produce its crops, and the Heavens will release the dew. Once more I will cause the remnant in Judah and Israel to inherit these blessings.*

You are blessed. The child in your womb is blessed. This is a time of favour, prosperity, and grace. God has goodness and excellence for your life. Though the world may seem to be in great turmoil and decline, the children of the Lord experience prosperity and peace.

Don't raise your child in fear or negativity. Her inheritance is pronounced plainly here in Zechariah. She is blessed with a life where she will be in the right place at the right time. She will succeed in her pursuits. Her life will not be one of anger, gossip, and bullies. Instead, it will be a life of strong friendships and peace.

Your child is a seed of prosperity and peace to your family. Her presence will bring harmony where there has been strife. Abundance will surround her. She will take hold of inheritances lost. She will acquire all that belongs to her. Your child will not be cheated of her rightful favour.

Confession and prayer: Father, thank You for the seed of peace, blessing, and prosperity You have placed in my womb.

Week 31: Day 5

Luke 1:41 (NLT) *At the sound of Mary's greeting, Elizabeth's child leaped within her, and Elizabeth was filled with the Holy Spirit.*

I pray that you have forged relationships with other mums-to-be. There is something special about being pregnant at the same time as someone else. Your children have the chance to be lifelong friends, and you have someone who knows exactly what you're going through.

At this stage in Mary's life, she possibly had no girlfriends with whom she could share her excitement. She came to see Elizabeth, perhaps with some apprehension as to whether she would be accepted, or told she was mad. But God had gone ahead of her, to the extent that not only was Elizabeth excited, so was her child.

Friendships are often based on common ground. Mary and Elizabeth both had miracle babies, who would grow up to be great men. Others may have mocked and criticised them, but they used their relationship to gain strength and courage. Motherhood has its challenges, so take time now to step out of your comfort zone and make new friends. Begin relationships with other mothers, where you will encourage and strengthen each other on your journey.

Confession and prayer: Father, help me to make lifelong friends with likeminded mothers, who will be an encouragement to me, and I to them.

Week 31: Day 6

Luke 1:46-47 (NLT) *Mary responded, "Oh, how my soul praises the Lord. How my spirit rejoices in God my Savior!"*

Yesterday we spoke about forming friendships with other pregnant mothers. If you are a first-time mother, this is probably easy for you to do. However, if this is your fourth child, for example, life is pretty full on, and connecting with other mothers is low on the to-do list. My advice: put it higher on that list. It will make you a better mother, and person, with girlfriends on your side.

God knew that Mary needed a friend in Elizabeth. He brought the two together because they understood each other. The age difference was great, but they taught and encouraged one another. They became great mothers, producing amazing sons because of their relationship. They praised God together, and they probably cried together too.

God knows that you need women who will spur you on to be a better mother. As He brought Mary and Elizabeth together, so He will lead you to exciting new friendships. At first, God's choice may seem odd, but you will be surprised how valuable she will become.

Confession and prayer: Father, I pray for friendships that will cause me to be a better person and mother.

Week 31: Day 7

James 5:10 (NLT) *For examples of patience in suffering, dear brothers and sisters, look at the prophets who spoke in the name of the Lord.*

Patience in suffering is perhaps not the most positive way to describe pregnancy, although it may be how some of you are feeling today. If you feel as though you are facing hardship, take heart, and be patient. Think of the prophets.

Old Testament prophets were an interesting bunch to say the least. They spoke God's warnings and calls to repentance. Virtually all were not liked for what they said, but were faithful to their call regardless. Many prophets did not see the fulfilment of their words. They waited in patience.

The child in your womb is like prophecy. She is a promise of a life unseen. She began as a seed, and one day you will see her burst forth. The good news for you is that you will see the fruition of your little prophecy, and you only have to wait a few more weeks. However, as with prophets of old, everything will happen in God's timing. Trust Him, be patient, your prophecy will be fulfilled. Don't rush things. God's timing is perfect.

Confession and prayer: God, I have patience as I wait for my child to be born.

Week 32: Day 1

1 Thessalonians 2:11 (NKJV) *As you know how we exhorted, and comforted, and charged every one of you, as a father does his own children.*

There are plenty of books out there that tell you how to raise the perfect child, but in my opinion, the best book for parenting advice is the Bible. Our Father in Heaven parents each of us perfectly, so if anyone knows how to treat your children, it is Him.

Thessalonians gives us three basic guides for parenthood: exhort, comfort, charge. Exhortation means to encourage and build someone up. To exhort your children means that you tell them how incredibly amazing they are. When you see your offspring as the most talented child you have ever known, and tell them so, you are practicing exhortation. It is not a bad thing. Remember, telling your friends how talented your child is, is not exhortation. You have to tell your child.

Secondly, Scripture talks about giving comfort. There will be times when your child needs comfort, and times when you will need to step back and give space to learn and grow. Wisdom will teach you the difference.

The last role of a parent as described in Thessalonians is to charge. This means to inspire and release your child in her destiny and purpose. It is an honour to shape and mould a child toward greatness. Nothing matches the awesomeness of being a parent.

Confession and prayer: Father, I model my parenting on You. I will exhort, comfort, and release my child into her purpose.

Week 32: Day 2

1 Corinthians 13:3 (NLT) *If I gave everything I have to the poor and even sacrificed my body, I could boast about it; but if I didn't love others, I would have gained nothing.*

There are many noble and noteworthy deeds in this life, but at the top of the list is love. Love is the action that trumps all others. It is greatest of all, conquers all, and will endure to the end.

One would think that as a parent, love is a no-brainer. Surely you don't need to tell a mother to love her children? Parental love towards her child is always present, but there are times that we need to be reminded to practice love for our family, above all else.

Giving all that you can to the poor, sacrificing your body, working late, and making more money to pay school fees is well and good, but what matters most to your children, is love. If they do not see your love for them in action, it will all be in vain. Demonstrate your love for your family above all endeavours.

Confession and prayer: God, I choose to put my family first and demonstrate my love for them.

Week 32: Day 3

1 Corinthians 13:4 (NLT) *Love is patient and kind. Love is not jealous or boastful or proud.*

When the baby you carry is placed in your arms for the first time, feelings of love will no doubt overwhelm you. How can one so small evoke such huge emotions? She is a gift!

Love is not just a feeling, it is an action. Most of the time, you will be so absorbed in love for your child, that actions of patience and kindness will naturally flow. But sometimes, love becomes a choice that is made on purpose. Yes, there will be times when you will be infuriated by your bundle of joy! It will be tempting to yell, and let anger rise.

Choose to be overly patient with your kids. Choose to show them kindness, more than the kindness you show a random stranger. Choose not to be jealous of what other children achieve. Love your child for who she is, not who you want her to be.

Exercise love in all its forms. Children can never be over-loved.

Confession and prayer: Even when I don't feel like it, I choose to love and demonstrate love.

Week 32: Day 4

1 Corinthians 13:7 (NLT) *Love never gives up, never loses faith, is always hopeful, and endures through every circumstance.*

As a child I wasn't overly affectionate. I hated being continually kissed and hugged. I would wriggle my way out. I wanted to be left alone. Now that I am the parent, things are different. I am the one who is constantly hugging and kissing my children. My love for them is beyond what I ever thought possible.

1 Corinthians 13:7 describes so perfectly the love I feel for my boys. It will never give up, lose faith, lose hope, but will continue through every circumstance. Nothing they do will stop me from loving them. That is the strength of my love.

I have done nothing to generate this kind of love . It is God's gift to every parent. The gift of enduring love. A gift for parents to treasure and share. Allow His gift of love for your child to overwhelm you.

Confession and prayer: Thank You, God, for the gift of enduring, steadfast love for my baby. I allow You to impart that love in my heart.

Week 32: Day 5

Romans 8:38-39 (NLT) *And I am convinced that nothing can ever separate us from God's love. Neither death nor life, neither angels nor demons, neither our fears for today nor our worries about tomorrow—not even the powers of hell can separate us from God's love. No power in the sky above or in the earth below—indeed, nothing in all creation will ever be able to separate us from the love of God that is revealed in Christ Jesus our Lord.*

Yesterday I spoke about the God-given gift of enduring love between a parent and child. We can love like that because He has loved us first. Father loves you with enduring, eternal love. Nothing you have ever done, or will do, can separate you from His love.

Your pregnancy may be the result of a one night stand, or an affair. That does not change God's mind about you. He loves you as much as ever. Jesus Christ revealed God's love to the world by dying in our place. He has taken your punishment. You don't need to punish yourself. Accept His love.

You may not believe that such love exists. After your baby is born, you will know that it does because you will experience it firsthand. In that moment, remember that God's love for you is even greater than the love you feel for your child. He loves you. Jesus loves you. More than you will ever know in this life.

Confession and prayer: Father, reveal Your love to me.

Week 32: Day 6

Psalm 118:17 (NLT) *I will not die; instead, I will live to tell what the Lord has done.*

Giving birth is dangerous. Having a baby is a natural process which women have been doing for centuries. However, this natural process can kill mothers and children, and it has done for centuries. I do not write this to invoke fear, but to remind you of the importance of confessing and declaring the Word. You and your baby will not die, but live to declare the goodness of God.

Whether you are having a textbook pregnancy, or things have been touch and go from the start, there are risks involved in childbirth. Obstetricians and health professionals will not be taking anything lightly when it comes to the welfare of you and baby. Neither should you. As written before, there is an enemy of humankind, and he wants nothing but to kill, steal, and destroy. Counteract by declaring promises of abundant life.

Childbirth is wrought with danger, yet in all things you and baby will not die; instead you will live to tell what the Lord has done.

Confession and prayer: God, I declare that in childbirth we will not die, we will live to testify of what You have done.

Week 32: Day 7

Philippians 1:9 (NLT) *I pray that your love will overflow more and more, and that you will keep on growing in knowledge and understanding.*

If you are already a parent, you will know that love for your child does not stop. From the moment she is born, love for her will grow and overflow, more and more. Love is not the only thing in life that should grow. Along with love, Paul prays that knowledge and understanding increase.

Parenting is one of the biggest jobs most of us undertake, yet few attempt to gain further understanding on the subject. Being a good parent is not something we are born with. It is a learned skill. That is good news, especially for those who did not grow up in a healthy home environment. Everyone can, and should aim to learn more about parenting.

Read books, attend seminars, and talk to other parents. You don't have to copy what others do, but glean from their experience. Just as love will continue to overflow for your child, be sure to allow your skills as a parent to grow and develop as well.

Confession and prayer: I will make the effort to grow as a parent. I am not afraid to ask for help or hone my parenting skills.

Week 33: Day 1

Psalm 112:1-2 (NLT) *Praise the Lord! How joyful are those who fear the Lord and delight in obeying his commands. Their children will be successful everywhere; an entire generation of godly people will be blessed.*

The Bible is full of promises that God makes to families. Psalm 112 is one of them. Many people pray this passage over their family every day.

The first promise that God makes is that your children will be successful and blessed. Never take promises like this for granted. God means every word He says. If He has promised to make your children successful, He will bring it to pass.

In years to come you may find that your child is struggling in an area at school. Pray and confess this Psalm over her life. Work with her and get the help she needs, but don't forget to take the problem to God. He has promised her success. Make demands on the Lord's promises in the spirit realm. This is how the Bible is a two-edged sword. Use it to your advantage when it comes to your children. Your baby is successful and blessed.

Confession and prayer: God, I believe that my children are successful and blessed according to Psalm 112.

Week 33: Day 2

Psalm 112:4 (NLT) *Light shines in the darkness for the godly. They are generous, compassionate, and righteous.*

When your family experiences dark times, the light of Jesus shines through. If you are going through dark times in your life today, allow the light of Christ to fill you. His light pierces through the darkness.

You may be facing one of the most challenging experiences of your life thus far. You might be thinking that a new baby will make matters worse. Rest assured that you will get through. God has allowed your baby to be born at this time to bring happiness and joy. She will be a delight in your desperate situation. Light shines in the darkness.

Don't allow bitterness to creep in. Continue to be generous, compassionate, and good to others. You will come through this time, so do it with grace. Arise, shine, for your Light has come, and He has birthed a new light in you. She will break through the dark times, and bring the most wonderful joy.

Confession and prayer: Lord, I look to Your light to bring hope in my situation.

Week 33: Day 3

Psalm 112:6 (NLT) *Such people will not be overcome by evil. Those who are righteous will be long remembered.*

Know this: evil will always be overcome by good. Righteous deeds will triumph over bad. Darkness will succumb to the light. The evil that has come against you will not prevail. The Cross has conquered all.

Those who are righteous will be remembered. The world celebrates notorious criminals, but children do not. Your baby needs a good mother and father, a stable home. She will be thankful that she had parents who gave her a good start. Her life will attest to your honesty and integrity.

Evil will not have the final word, it is the life of the righteous that will be recognised for generations to come. Your child will have fond memories of your kindness and loving heart. It is not boring or conservative to be righteous. Being a goodie-goodie is outstanding. God has made you upright. Set an example for your child, and don't allow evil to overcome you.

Confession and prayer: God, I believe that You will never allow evil to overcome my family.

Week 33: Day 4

Psalm 112:7 (NLT) *They do not fear bad news; they confidently trust the Lord to care for them.*

Bad news is all around. From media to lunchroom gossip, there is no shortage of bad news. But for those who have put their hope in God, things are looking up. Bad news may abound, but when God of the Angel Armies is looking after you, there is nothing to fear.

Trust in the Lord's protection for you and your family. He has angels that guard and protect. They are on duty twenty-four hours a day. God will not allow harm to come near you.

Many of David's psalms begin in lament as David prays about those who plan destruction against him. In most cases, the psalm finishes with words of triumph and hope. David recalls that God has never let him down in the past, and isn't going to start now. You may like to read a few psalms today, and be encouraged that God will take care of you. It may not always be roses, but you will find peace.

Confession and prayer: Father, I trust in You to care for me and my family. You will never let us down.

Week 33: Day 5

Psalm 112:8 (NLT) *They are confident and fearless and can face their foes triumphantly.*

This is one of the last family blessings of Psalm 112, a life of confidence and triumph. Children are naturally confident, and believe they are winners. Life experience wears such self belief away. As a parent you can re-inject your child with confidence and the anticipation of victory.

The role of a parent is to love and encourage her children. Never tell your child that she is a failure. Never humiliate her for her mistakes. Don't put her down or make her feel worthless. She already has enough to contend with. She does not need your judgement or criticism.

Your words are powerful in the life of your offspring. Use them to create a confident child, who believes she is a winner. When things aren't going her way, may you be the only one cheering her on. She will conquer any foe when she knows that her parents are backing her all the way.

Confession and prayer: Father, I promise that I will use my words to praise and install confidence in my child.

Week 33: Day 6

Philippians 4:8 (NLT) *And now, dear brothers and sisters, one final thing. Fix your thoughts on what is true, and honorable, and right, and pure, and lovely, and admirable. Think about things that are excellent and worthy of praise.*

As a child, my sister experienced graphic nightmares. My father would pray this verse with her each night. He would pray that her dreams would be of things true, honourable, right, pure, lovely, and admirable. After she stopped having nightmares, the prayer was so comforting to her that they would pray it together, even when she was a teen.

I now pray a similar prayer over my children each night before they sleep. I pray that they will dream of lovely and excellent things. That they dream of Heaven and Jesus.

Our bodies need good sleep. Frequent nightmares and bad dreams do not lead to serene slumber. In fact, they can cause a fear of sleep, along with other problems. It is horrible for parents to listen to their child cry out in terror through the night. For your sake, and hers, you want your child to sleep well, and have good dreams. Use this Scripture to pray that she will have excellent and lovely dreams.

Confession and prayer: Father, I pray that my baby will dream of excellent and wonderful things from the times she is born.

Week 33: Day 7

Ruth 4:14 (CEV) *After his birth, the women said to Naomi: Praise the LORD! Today he has given you a grandson to take care of you. We pray that the boy will grow up to be famous everywhere in Israel.*

I grew up with the privilege of both maternal and paternal grandparents being close by. They were very much a part of my life, even as an adult, until they passed away. Grandparents are special people for your child. It is wonderful for older people to have young children in their lives.

Naomi cherished being a grandmother. I imagine her being doting to the point of embarrassment. Perhaps Naomi reminds you of someone!

I am sure that Naomi constantly talked about her grandson. He was probably all she talked about. The two would have created many wonderful memories together. Most importantly, Naomi taught her grandchild God's goodness. After all, he was a testament to the Almighty's greatness.

Cherish your child's grandparents. Yes, they will spoil her, and let her get away with far more than you ever could, but that is what grandparents are for. Enjoy them!

Confession and prayer: Father, thank You for my baby's grandparents.

Week 34: Day 1

Psalm 51:6 (NLT) *But you desire honesty from the womb, teaching me wisdom even there.*

Right now you are very aware that your baby is growing every day. Your abdomen is no doubt quite cramped! While still in your womb, God is giving your baby special lessons in wisdom and truth. She is growing spiritually too.

Father God teaches babies wisdom and honesty in the womb. That is why newborns seem to be so pure and innocent. They have been immersed in honesty and godliness. Expressions and movements of your child that melt your heart, are due to the purity of Heaven that she has been taught.

Children are born with the ability to be truthful, and make good decisions. We are led to believe that our sinful nature puts us on the back foot. The Bible says that God teaches us wisdom in the innermost parts. He gives us every possible chance to succeed and be wise. Being wise and honest is innate. God has placed these qualities inside every baby, including yours. Encourage her to practice this purity and overcome temptation.

Confession and prayer: Father, thank You for teaching my baby to be truthful and wise.

Week 34: Day 2

Psalm 31:24 (MSG) *Be brave. Be strong. Don't give up. Expect God to get here soon.*

With around six weeks to go until baby is born, you may be feeling both excitement, and apprehension. What will this labour be like? Will it be painful? Whatever happens: be brave, be strong, don't give up.

This should be a mantra that plays through your head in the birthing suite: God has made me brave and strong. Keep going. (Receive pain medication if necessary!) God is here, and He will help me deliver a healthy baby.

You can do this. You are an amazing woman, resilient and energetic. There may be some pain and discomfort, but joy will arrive soon enough. It is your time to shine. Be brave, be strong. Expect God.

Of course, this applies to other areas of our lives. Whatever you are facing, remember this verse: Be brave, be strong, don't give up. Expect God to show up soon, because He certainly will. He always does.

Confession and prayer: I am brave and strong. I don't give up. I expect God to show up in my situation.

Week 34: Day 3

Psalm 91:1-2 (NLT) *Those who live in the shelter of the Most High will find rest in the shadow of the Almighty. This I declare about the Lord: He alone is my refuge, my place of safety; he is my God, and I trust him.*

To me, a baby, living and growing in the womb, is a secret place. Despite the best imaging techniques, no one can truly see your child, but the Most High. As she rests in His shadow, her spirit is learning to trust Him. She knows Him as her refuge and safety.

What a privilege for your baby to be in the secret place of God. Such a beautiful place to be. No wonder many babies (at least my babies) don't like to arrive on time but prefer to stay in utero for a few days longer. Who would want to give up being in the secret place of the Most High?

You might like to talk to your baby about her secret place. Encourage her to cherish these moments. Remind her that while she is in a secure place right now, the Lord will continue to be her refuge after she is born. She can always find Him in the secret place of her heart. The Almighty is her God.

Confession and prayer: Father, watch over my baby in Your secret place. May she find rest in Your shadow.

Week 34: Day 4

Psalm 91:3 (NLT) *For he will rescue you from every trap and protect you from deadly disease.*

Thanks to advances in medical science, some diseases that were once deadly have vanished from modern society. But there are still illnesses that can take a child's life.
Compared to a century ago, doctors and scientists have identified many more diseases. It seems that we take two steps forward, and two steps back.

Your child will be exposed to all manner of toxins and microbes. No matter how diligent you are, or whether you immunise your child, they will not be protected from every fatal illness.

Only God can provide full protection against deadly disease. He can and will. The Most High will protect your child from diseases that threaten her life. It is His promise.

If ever you are in a situation where your baby is threatened by a deadly illness, trust in God. He has promised to rescue her. You don't need to fear. His protection is fail safe.

Confession and prayer: Father, I trust You to protect my child from every deadly disease.

Week 34: Day 5

Psalm 91:4 (NLT) *He will cover you with his feathers. He will shelter you with his wings. His faithful promises are your armour and protection.*

The protection of the Lord is not harsh or burdensome. He covers us with feathers. He covers your child with feathers. His promises offer gentle protection. His wings hide us from trouble.

Often we think of God as powerful, strong, and mighty. But He is also gentle, with soft feathers, and beautiful wings. He gently caresses your baby with His feathers. He strokes her face with His pinions. What a lovely picture! Right now, she rests in the shelter of His soft wings. She is cocooned in His loving embrace. What could come against her? What could get through such secure, yet peaceful protection?

You can be sure that the Word of God is true. He will keep you safe. His promises are protection. You can rely on Him. Allow His feathers to stroke your heart and bring peace. His promises for you and baby are a refuge of safety.

Confession and prayer: God, I delight in Your gentleness, and the peace that it brings to me and my unborn child.

Psalm 91:5-7 (NLT) *Do not be afraid of the terrors of the night, nor the arrow that flies in the day. Do not dread the disease that stalks in darkness, nor the disaster that strikes at midday. Though a thousand fall at your side, though ten thousand are dying around you, these evils will not touch you.*

Your God is big. No, wait, He is huge. And He makes massive promises. Because He is so tremendous, He can keep them. That is the God you and I serve.

There are all manner of things that will come against your child in her lifetime. There is an enemy that wants to destroy her soul. God is bigger than that. Whatever it is, she will be untouched. She is untouchable.

Dreams may threaten her in the night, but she will be untouched. Arrows will attempt to pierce her heart and break her spirit, she will be untouched. Diseases may lurk and stalk around, she will be untouched. Disaster may strike, she will be untouched. All this may happen in one day, yet no harm will come near. Everyone else may be falling, she will not be affected. This is the Lord's promise to your child, and His promise to you.

Confession and prayer: Father, thank You for protecting my baby. Even if everyone else experiences trouble, I know You are looking after her.

Week 34: Day 7

Psalm 91:9-11 (NLT) *If you make the Lord your refuge, if you make the Most High your shelter, no evil will conquer you; no plague will come near your home. For he will order his angels to protect you wherever you go.*

Even people who don't necessarily believe in God, ascribe to the belief in guardian angels. After all, having a supernatural being looking after you is a nice thought. Guardian angles are real. They are not just supernatural bodyguards. They have a divine assignment given form the God of Heaven. They aren't pretty cherubs that can sit on your shoulder, they are warriors, backed by the Almighty.

There are angles assigned to you and your baby. They have been ordered by God. Their job is to make sure that the will of God is fulfilled.

It warms a parent's heart to know there are angels watching over her children. What God promises in Psalm 91 is so much more than that. Your baby has an angel assigned to her, making sure no evil comes near, protecting her from harm. And if necessary, your child's angel will call on others to assist in grave danger.

Every parent wants to protect her child, but when you can't be there, or when it is beyond you, The Lord has sent His angel. Make demand's on the Lord's angels. They are ordered to protect.

Confession and prayer: Lord God, thank You for the angels you have assigned to protect, and watch over my baby.

Week 35: Day 1

Psalm 91:14-16 (NLT) *The Lord says, "I will rescue those who love me. I will protect those who trust in my name. When they call on me, I will answer; I will be with them in trouble. I will rescue and honor them. I will reward them with a long life and give them my salvation."*

Psalm 91:14-16 in the New International Version reads:
"Because he loves me," says the Lord, "I will rescue him; I will protect him, for he acknowledges my name. He will call on me, and I will answer him; I will be with him in trouble, I will deliver him, and honour him. With long life I will satisfy him and show him my salvation."
Because he loves me... The most important thing you can teach your baby is to love God. Who cares when she rolls over, walks, or talks. They all do eventually. What matters most is that she loves Jesus.

The Lord makes wonderful promises to those who love Him. He promises to rescue and protect. He promises to answer prayer. He promises to be with those who love Him, and that they will be rewarded. However, to me, the most important promise is the last: a long life and the experience of salvation, with eternal life.

Your baby has been created to love God. We all have. Teach her to love Him though your own love relationship. Your child will grow and learn, but do not forsake the most important thing. She has been made to love God.

Confession and prayer: Father, I love You. I will teach my child to love You, and enjoy Your salvation.

Week 35: Day 2

Job 27:3 (NLT) *As long as I live, while I have breath from God.*

Every breath you breathe, every breath your baby takes, is from God. He gives breath and He gives life. Job experienced many horrible things, yet He knew to thank God for every breath.

Some babies are born with breathing difficulties. Others suffer frequent respiratory infection. God does not take breath away. He gives breath. The devil will attempt to steal life and breath, God gives it in abundance.

If your baby needs a respirator when she is born, or if she struggles with breathing at any time in her life, remember that God gives breath. You do not need to worry or be afraid. Every breath she breathes is from God. He does not give sparingly, He always gives in abundance. Your child will breathe and have life. Her breath is from God. His Spirit fills her lungs. He has blessed her with the gift of life, the gift of breath.

Confession and prayer: God, I know that when my child is born, You will breathe life into her.

Week 35: Day 3

Isaiah 54:17a (NLT) *But in that coming day no weapon turned against you will succeed.*

The devil has all manner of weapons in his arsenal. He has come against you, using all kinds of strategies in the past. Before your baby has been born, he has attempted to attack her as well. But his attacks are in vain. No weapon formed against you shall prosper.

Satan is relentless. You defeat him one day, but that does not mean he will give in. Day after day he will drop thoughts into your head, that can steal your happiness, and destroy your life. Do not let him. Do not let any weapons that form against you prosper.

The Word says it, but it is your job to lay hold of it. Satan will keep forming weapons to bring you down, do not allow them to prosper in your life.

The same is true for your child. Throughout her life he will fashion weapons against her, some will be minor, others deadly. No weapon formed against her shall prosper. Never give the devil an inch. No weapon means exactly that.

Confession and prayer: The devil may be relentless, but I will stand on the promise that no weapon formed against me, or my family, will prosper.

Week 35: Day 4

Ephesians 2:10 (NLT) *For we are God's masterpiece. He has created us anew in Christ Jesus, so we can do the good things he planned for us long ago.*

You have a masterpiece inside you. Isn't that wonderful? A masterpiece. From the tips of her fingers, to her gorgeous toes, she is the most incredible masterpiece you will lay eyes on. She is divinely unique and special.

But it does not stop there. God does not just create masterpieces. He creates masterpieces that do good. It is important that children know Ephesians 2:10 in its entirety. If a child believes she is a masterpiece, she will be self-centred, and expect the world to revolve around her. She is more than a masterpiece, she has good works to do.

Yes, your baby is a masterpiece, but she has also been created to do good to others. God has prepared much for her to accomplish. Part of being a masterpiece is using the mastery of talents she has to make the world a better place. Remind her often that she is God's masterpiece, and remind her that she can demonstrate that to the world by doing good.

Confession and prayer: Father, thank You for the amazing masterpiece inside me. She has been created wonderfully, to do good things for others.

Week 35: Day 5

Psalm 150:6 (AMP) *Let everything that has breath and every breath of life praise the Lord! Praise the Lord! (Hallelujah!)*

Children love to praise the Lord. It is amazing that as babies, before they can even speak, children will respond positively to music that praises God. We have been created to magnify our Creator.

Psalm 150:6 is not just a statement, it is a command. It commands everything that has breath, and every breath of life to praise the Lord. When your baby exits the womb, and takes her first breath, she is praising God. Her lungs will erupt with screams and cries. She is praising God.

If you face a different picture. If your baby is born blue and struggling to breathe, command her to praise the Lord with her breath according to Psalm 150. Speak to her body, tell her that she has God's breath of life. Encourage her to praise her Maker. Explain her impending birth, and that as she takes a breath for the first time, she will praise God with her voice. Confess that she will not experience respiratory complications but that she will immediately praise God.

Confession and prayer: I believe that my baby will praise God with her lungs and voice as soon as she is born.

Week 35: Day 6

Romans 8:28 (NLT) *And we know that God causes everything to work together for the good of those who love God and are called according to his purpose for them.*

God has nothing but good things in store for you and your baby. He will work every situation into a good one. You may experience bad things. They are not the work of God. But God can do more than leave you with bad situations. He will turn them into good. No other god is like that. He's pretty amazing!

Let's think about your labour and birth. No one knows for certain how things are going to turn out. You may get the birth you have been praying and believing for, or not. The devil is out to steal, kill, and destroy. He will attempt to sabotage things, and your baby's birth may not be so great.

That is not the end of the story. The devil may make a mess, God will turn it into good. God loves you. He loves your baby. He will turn everything around for good. You will hold a healthy, beautiful baby. It will be all good.

Confession and prayer: Father, I believe that You turn all things in my life around for good.

Week 35: Day 7

James 1:12 (NLT) *God blesses those who patiently endure testing and temptation. Afterward they will receive the crown of life that God has promised to those who love him.*

Some people are in labour for a few minutes, and then the baby pops out. I think it tends to happen that way once you have had a few children already. For others, labour is all about patience and endurance. Once you have endured until the end, you will lovingly embrace a beautiful baby. It will all be worth it.

When a contraction hits, you probably won't be thinking about Scripture. You will work through whatever coping strategies you can to manage the intensity. That is why it is a good idea to fill your mind with the Word now. Tell your body that it can endure to the end. That it can overcome the force of any contraction. You can endure this one minute of pain (the average duration of a contraction), knowing the end result is the greatest prize, a baby.

In the lead up to your due date keep confessing and meditating on the Word. Your body will endure. The Lord will be your helper. Keep the prize in sight. After you have endured, your child will be in your arms.

Confession and prayer: Body, you are strong enough to endure the labour and birth of this baby.

Week 36: Day 1

Psalm 103:1-2 (NLT) *Let all that I am praise the Lord; with my whole heart, I will praise his holy name. Let all that I am praise the Lord; may I never forget the good things he does for me.*

Everyone has bad days. Everyone goes through times in their lives when things don't work out. At those times it is easy to forget the good things God has done. Consumed by the negative, God can be where we lay the blame. We have forgotten to praise. Good things are a distant memory.

The psalmist says, "May I never forget the good things He does for me." May you never forget the good things God does for you. No matter how tough it gets. No matter how bad things are.

You are roughly 36 weeks pregnant. In a few weeks you will hold a gorgeous new baby. What a joy. Such a blessing. A good thing.

There are many couples who envy your position. Many who are so desperate to be pregnant. Your pregnancy is a good thing, and your baby is an even better thing. When things get too hard to handle, look at your baby, and may you never forget the good things God has done.

Confession and prayer: Father, I praise You for the good thing You have done by enabling me to fall pregnant with this baby.

Week 36: Day 2

Psalm 103:3-4 (NLT) *He forgives all my sins and heals all my diseases. He redeems me from death and crowns me with love and tender mercies.*

You are forgiven and redeemed from death. The punishment for sin is death, but if Jesus Christ is Lord of your life, you are redeemed. Take a moment to celebrate that. You and I will not be punished for our sin. Praise God!

This verse is not just talking about eternal death. Father has redeemed your life from physical death. You will not die before your time. Neither will your baby.

Never take anything for granted. In some parts of the world mothers and babies often die during birth. But the hand of God is at work keeping babies alive. He has redeemed your baby from death. She will not die.

Redemption from death is one of the benefits of praising the Lord and being a believer. In place of death, God promises a crown of love and tender mercy. Your child already wears a crown. He has crowned her with life. You and baby are redeemed from death.

Confession and prayer: Father, thank You for redeeming me and my baby from death, and for crowning us with life instead.

Week 36: Day 3

Psalm 103:5a (NLT) *He fills my life with good things.*

Life is full of good things. Look around right now. God has placed many good things in your life. People, possessions, dreams, career - all good things He has positioned in life to enjoy.

Your baby will be a source of joy and happiness when she is born. For some women however, happiness is replaced with depression. Postnatal depression is often due to a number of small things becoming overwhelming. I am not going to suggest a method for overcoming postnatal depression, that is the job of a medical professional. But here is a little thing, that you can add to other little things suggested by professionals, that will help: Praise God for the good things.

God has filled your life with good things. There may be a time when it is difficult to recognise this, but it is in those times that you need to practice Psalm 103. Praise Him for the good things, praise Him for your child. Praise Him for the (at times little) sleep you had last night. Praise Him for friendship. It is a little thing that can pull you from one day to the next. It could even be the key to healing.

Confession and prayer: Father, help me to always recognise the good things You have placed in my life. I will forever praise You.

Week 36: Day 4

Psalm 103:5 (NLT) *He fills my life with good things. My youth is renewed like the eagle's!*

Life is certainly full of good things. Ice cream, coffee, chocolate, friends, holidays, family, babies, and more. And the best part is that God renews our youth so we can enjoy them for longer.

Think about that for a moment: if life wasn't full of good things, what would be the point of living long? Who would want to live a youthful life when bad things constantly happen? If life is awful, you want to keel over and die!

Have you noticed this to be true? It seems to me that those who live unpleasant lives, age quicker than those whose lives are full of goodness. No one wants to live a long life filled with pain.

So how do you stay youthful to keep up with your kids? Make good choices, follow the Lord, and let His goodness chase after you. Acknowledge and praise Him for His blessings, and your youth will be renewed like the eagle's. You will live a long life without pain, looking much younger than you really are!

Confession and prayer: Father, thank You for keeping me young!

Week 36: Day 5

Psalm 103:13 (NLT) *The Lord is like a father to his children, tender and compassionate to those who fear him.*

The biggest misconception in the world today is that God is angry and judgemental towards humanity. Unfortunately, Christians are largely to blame for this error. The truth is that God is the opposite: tender and compassionate. His anger and judgement was placed on Jesus when He bore our sin on the cross. God is not angry. He is full of love toward His children.

I encourage you to get to know God as He is. In other words, study Scripture to see your Heavenly Father as loving and merciful. The more you know God to be a Father of love and goodness, the more you will model this behaviour in your life, and with your own children.

If you want to be an amazing parent, imitate Father God. He is not a God of anger or scolding, but rather a God of compassion and tenderness. Don't continue the misconception with your children. Be a parent of love and kindness, thus teaching them that their Father in Heaven is exactly the same.

Confession and prayer: Father, I meditate on Your love and mercy. That is the image of You I present to the world and my children.

Week 36: Day 6

Psalm 103:17-18 (NLT) *But the love of the Lord remains forever with those who fear him. His salvation extends to the children's children of those who are faithful to his covenant, of those who obey His commandments!*

There is no doubt about it, God thinks generationally. He is the God of Abraham, Isaac and Jacob. He blesses entire family lines. He is not just interested in you, but also the generations that will come from your descendants.

While you may be starting your family, it is never too early to think even further into the future. For most people, the only thoughts of their future is monetary. That's well and good, but God's plans for generations exceed money. His blessings include salvation, healing, prosperity, and favour.

So how do you prepare for that kind of future? Start by praying. Talk to the Lord about His vision for your children, and their children. Make teaching your children about the Lord a priority. Establish godliness in your progeny. Live a gracious life before God, and you will see the fulfilment of this psalm, where His salvation extends to your offspring, and theirs.

Confession and prayer: Father, help me establish a godly legacy for my children and my children's children.

Week 36: Day 7

Psalm 103:20-21 (NLT) *Praise the Lord, you angels, you mighty ones who carry out his plans, listening for each of his commands. Yes, praise the Lord, you armies of angels who serve him and do his will!*

Would you like to have an army of supernatural beings at your disposal? That spring to action at your word? You can. You can, if you know how, and Psalm 103 gives us the key.

Angels serve God and do His will. They hearken to the plans of God ensuring that they are accomplished in the earth. How do you or I give angels assignments? By speaking God's will. Angles do not go to work when they hear God's voice, they work when they hear His will. So if you or I speak the Lord's will, angels will get to work, carrying out His commands. God's voice, your voice, as long as you speak His will, it makes no difference. Angels have to act.

What is God's will? His Word. You give angels assignments when you speak the Bible. When they hear the Word of God, they carry it out.

When it comes to your children (or any situation), pray and speak the Word of God. As you do angels are sent on assignment to bring it to fruition.

Confession and prayer: Father, I will not just speak my words, but will use Your Word to send angels on assignment.

Week 37: Day 1

Psalm 48:6 (NKJV) *Fear took hold of them there, and pain, as of a woman in birth pangs.*

Four weeks to go! This is, as some would say, the business end of pregnancy. Your baby and body are preparing for the final phase. Soon you will be the mother of a new little person living on the outside.

As you mentally prepare for giving birth do not let fear overtake you. Be strong. The psalmist describes what happens when fear takes hold - pain. If you want to avoid a painful birthing experience, don't be afraid.

Fear gives way to pain. Physiologically, emotions of fear release hormones that will heighten the pain you experience in labour. Science proves Scripture to be true!

Stay positive. Focus on the outcome: that your baby will soon be born. You can get through each contraction. Contractions are not bad, they cause your child to be born. They are not to be feared. Allow love and faith to replace thoughts and feelings of fear. You are an overcomer!

Confession and prayer: I will not allow fear to get the better of me during labour.

Week 37: Day 2

Matthew 17:20 (NLT) *"You don't have enough faith," Jesus told them. "I tell you the truth, if you had faith even as small as a mustard seed, you could say to this mountain, 'Move from here to there,' and it would move. Nothing would be impossible."*

In these final weeks, it is more important than ever to watch what you say. Keep confessing the promises you have received from the Lord regarding your pregnancy, birth, and baby. Hang around people who will encourage you. Stay away from those who will plant doubt in your heart. You shall have what you say.

To some, elements of giving birth can be a mountain. Perhaps your first child was born by caesarean section. Your mountain is to have a natural birth this time. Or maybe you child was born prematurely, so your mountain is to get as close to full term as possible. Whatever it is, keep speaking, keep believing, and you shall have whatsoever you say. That is God's promise, and He does not lie.

Speak to your mountain, and do not doubt. What you are facing may seem impossible. That is God's specialty. He will bring to pass that which you say.

Confession and prayer: Father, I speak to the mountain I face regarding my baby. I tell every mountain to be removed from my life. I do not doubt. I thank You, Jesus, that I have received what I say.

Week 37: Day 3

Luke 24:38 (NLT) *"Why are you frightened?" he asked. "Why are your hearts filled with doubt?"*

Doubt and fear. Small words, yet the number one reason you will not receive what you are believing for. Determine to rid your life of fear and doubt.

The context of Luke 24 is the resurrection. Jesus hung on a cross, then He appeared before them. They should be celebrating and embracing, instead they were full of panic and anxiety. The disciples had probably spent those past days when Jesus was in the grave, meditating on doubt and fear. When the Good News appeared before their eyes, they could not respond appropriately.

Keep God's promises and His Word before your eyes constantly over the next few days and weeks. Don't allow dread, frustration, or misgiving to consume you. So what if your baby is well overdue. Stay peaceful. Then, when the good news arrives, or is about to arrive, you will not respond in fear and doubt. You will respond in faith and love.

Confession and prayer: Lord, I meditate on faith and love. I remain peaceful for when my good news comes.

Week 37: Day 4

Psalm 27:3 (MSG) *When besieged, I'm calm as a baby. When all hell breaks loose, I'm collected and cool.*

We all know the saying, "She's sleeping like a baby." Unfortunately, not all babies are aware of this adage, and sleep soundly. Sleep is not something that naturally comes to all babies. Of course, there are babies who do everything on cue, hardly fuss, and sleep, well, like a baby. Then there are others who are sensitive, and needy of attention.

If your baby is more like the latter than the former, sleep, and other things, may be challenging. I especially like The Message translation of Psalm 27:3. Babies are supposed to be calm. Speak this Scripture over your child, and claim that she will be as calm as a baby! Her temperament may be quite sensitive, but you can train her to be calm, and take change in her stride.

One thing I have noticed is that babies and toddlers read their parents emotions, and act accordingly. If mum is getting flustered, and feeling hot under the collar, children act that way too. On the other hand, a calm mother helps bring peace to her children. So perhaps while you're speaking this Scripture over your child, you may do well to remind yourself that when all hell breaks loose, you stay collected and cool too.

Confession and prayer: When all hell breaks loose, I am collected and cool, and so is my baby.

Week 37: Day 5

Job 33:4 (NLT) *For the Spirit of God has made me, and the breath of the Almighty gives me life.*

The world today denies the existence of God. Educational institutions have eradicated the idea of God from all areas of learning. The Bible, prayer, and Jesus have been replaced with inclusive language and political correctness.

Parent, it is your job to teach your baby where she came from. Teach her while she is young that the Spirit of God made her, that His breath gives her life. She will not learn this at school, she will learn it from you.

There is such power in a child knowing she has been created by the Almighty. That the God of all Heaven, who loves her, cared enough to breathe life into her bones. It brings confidence and strength. Others may laugh and mock your baby's faith and belief, but this knowledge of her Creator will provide a sure foundation to build her life upon. She has been created by the Spirit of God, and His breath gives her life.

Confession and prayer: Father, I will teach my child that You formed her, and gave her life.

2 Corinthians 4:18 (NIV) *So we fix our eyes not on what is seen, but on what is unseen. For what is seen is temporary, but what is unseen is eternal.*

It is often the little things that cause life to unravel. Burnt toast, a malfunctioning computer, and being late for work, are all examples of little things that can bring about a meltdown. But they are temporary. They don't matter. We know not to fix our eyes there, and let them get us down, but we do. 2 Corinthians reminds us to lift our eyes to gaze on what matters, eternity.

Now think of this verse in relation to your impending labour. Fixing your thoughts on the pain will not get you anywhere. Well actually, it will. It will get even more pain. Pain is temporary, it is the seen. Instead, fix your thoughts on what is currently unseen, your baby. She is the eternal prize you are working towards. Lift up your eyes. Refuse to be overwhelmed with the temporary. Keep your eyes on the unseen. She will be here before you know it!

Confession and prayer: In every situation I refuse to get caught up in the temporary, little things. I choose to fix my eyes on the eternal.

Week 37: Day 7

Genesis 2:7 (NLT) *Then the LORD God formed the man from the dust of the ground. He breathed the breath of life into the man's nostrils, and the man became a living person.*

The creative power of the Almighty is incredible. He forms each and every person. Gives them distinct features. And at the moment of birth, He breathes life into lungs. Nothing happens by chance or fluke. His Spirit is there at delivery, breathing life into each little one.

When it is time for your child to be born, anticipate God's presence. He has been forming her body in the womb for almost nine months now, His Spirit will also be there at her birth. When she takes her first breath, it is because He breathed life into her. Her lungs will fill with His breath.

Giving birth is a mighty miracle. There is hard work involved, but a great reward in the end. When you hold a beautiful baby in your arms, think about the miracle that occurred. God was there with you all the way. He breathed life into your baby, and now He looks upon your new little family, and smiles.

Confession and prayer: Thank You, Father, for breathing life into my baby's lungs.

Week 38: Day 1

Psalm 1:3 (NLT) *They are like trees planted along the riverbank, bearing fruit each season. Their leaves never wither, and they prosper in all they do.*

Psalm 1 is a great psalm. Perhaps one of your favourites. To paraphrase the first two verses of Psalm 1, "Oh the joys of those who follow after God and meditate on His Word." Verse three then begins to list those joys. One of them is that you bear fruit in season.

Let's apply this to pregnancy. The average gestation for a human baby is forty weeks. You have been given a due date, a season, if you will, when your child should be born. The Bible says that if you delight in the Lord, you will bear fruit in season. Speak this over your body. Proclaim that your child will not be born prematurely, or overdue. She will be born in season.

Doctors do not like women progressing through pregnancy much longer than forty weeks. If having babies overdue is in your family line, speak this Scripture in faith. Declare that your child will be born in season, and that you will not need to be induced. You bear fruit in season.

Confession and prayer: Lord, I declare that my baby will be born in her due season. I will not need to be induced.

Week 38: Day 2

Genesis 3:16a (NLT) *Then he said to the woman, "I will sharpen the pain of your pregnancy, and in pain you will give birth."*

Pain. As a result of the curse, women bear children in pain. If only Eve did not eat from the tree. If only the curse could be reversed. If only there was a way for women to deliver children pain free (I mean without an epidural).

There is. Jesus reversed the curse. He struck the serpent's head. He has overcome the curse by becoming the curse for us. Jesus has made a way. Read Galatians 3:13. He took the curse.

You don't have to suffer under the curse of experiencing pain in childbirth. Jesus paid the price, all you have to do is walk in His freedom.

Contractions help your baby into the world, pain does not. You can experience contractions without experiencing pain. Jesus bore the pain of your childbirth on the Cross. Your child's delivery can be different. It can come about without pain. Believe and you will receive.

Confession and prayer: I do not accept the curse of pain as part of my childbirth experience.

Week 38: Day 3

Luke 6:38 (NKJV) *Give, and it will be given to you: good measure, pressed down, shaken together, and running over will be put into your bosom. For with the same measure that you use, it will be measured back to you.*

Breast feeding is a slightly controversial issue for many mothers. For some women, breast feeding comes naturally, for others it is a struggle. Whatever you choose to do with regards to feeding your baby, feel comfortable with your choice. You have chosen what is best for you and your child.

It is amazing the keys that you find in Scripture, yes, even for breast feeding. Jesus said, "Give and it will be given into your bosom." There's a tip for breast feeding mothers! Our bodies work according to principles from the Bible. If you want to supply your baby with plenty of milk, so much it is overflowing, give her milk. The more you give, the more you will find flowing back into your bosom.

Breast feeding can be stressful for mother and baby. Seek help from a midwife who is gentle and supportive. When done properly it should not cause discomfort. And then feed your baby, and give her milk often. Because as you give, it will be given to you, good measure, pressed down, shaken together, into your bosom.

Confession and prayer: Jesus, I believe that breast feeding will not be a problem for me, and that as I give, a good measure will be given back into my bosom.

Week 38: Day 4

Isaiah 66:8 (NIV) *Yet no sooner is Zion in labor than she gives birth to her children.*

This is God's desire for you. He desires that you will have a fast and vigorous birth. You don't need to be in labour for hours, or even days. Nine months of carrying a child is long enough! When you go into labour you don't want it dragging on. Believe in faith for a fast delivery.

Never limit God according to experience. Other friends (even Christians) may have experienced long and horrific labours. God is not limited to human experience. He surpasses that. Don't accept the status quo. Believe God for more.

And if it doesn't happen? Don't let it stop you from believing for better things next time. Don't question that other people will experience fast, pain-fee births. God has made a way through Jesus. He took the curse.

Have faith. God has the very best in His plan for your life. If you want a fast delivery, it is not impossible. Believe and don't doubt.

Confession and prayer: God, I refuse to limit You to my experience. I believe for a fast and pain-free delivery.

Week 38: Day 5

1 Chronicles 4:9 (NLT) *There was a man named Jabez who was more honorable than any of his brothers. His mother named him Jabez because his birth had been so painful.*

Every child's birth is unique. Your labour may go perfectly to plan, or it may be a frightening experience. Whatever happens in the birthing suite, don't let it define your offspring, or your motherhood. It is such a small part of life with your child. If it is amazing, fantastic; if not, move on. There are far more glorious moments for you and your child than her labour.

A topic at new mothers' groups is often labour. Some mothers will tell their story, whether sensational or horrific, as if it is a trophy to hang in the den. My advice is to avoid this kind of behaviour. Your child does not need to hear the gory details of how she entered the world. Instead, focus on the hand of God on her life throughout your pregnancy. Let her know that your loving arms were there to embrace her the instant she emerged. Remind her that the Spirit of God breathed life into her lungs as she took her first breath. She was never, and will never be a pain to you.

I wonder the response you will get if you paint this kind of picture of your baby's birth at mothers' group!

Confession and prayer: My baby will never be a pain to me. I will remind her of the good things about her birth.

Week 38: Day 6

Psalm 29:11 (NLT) *God makes his people strong. God gives his people peace.*

Labour and delivery are some of the most physically intense situations a woman will ever face. They will draw on resources, muscles and mental energy that you never knew you had. If you ever have need of God's strength and peace, it is during labour and delivery. Nice to know that you have it, hey?

There is great simplicity in Psalm 29:11. Sometimes we complicate things. Labour and delivery can be like that. Worrying can cause straightforward things to be blown out of proportion. God is telling you to keep things simple. He has all the strength you need. He has all the peace necessary for this time. Vanish fear and unbelief. Eradicate negativity. He has made you capable, and given you His composure. Peace that passes all understanding. Strength that can bend a bow of bronze.

Get back to the simple. Rest in His promise: He has made you strong, He has given you peace.

Confession and prayer: Father, I strip away the complicated, and get back to the basics. You have made me strong, and given me peace. I take that into the labour and delivery of my baby.

Week 38: Day 7

John 16:21(CEV) *When a woman is about to give birth, she is in great pain. But after it is all over, she forgets the pain and is happy, because she has brought a child into the world.*

As of tomorrow you have two weeks to go. Technically, your baby can be born anytime now, and will be considered healthy and full term. You may be praying that this is so. For the majority, you still have a few days (or dare I say, weeks) left. Don't despair, your time will come.

Soon, you will be the woman that John 16:21 is talking about. Yes, during labour and delivery you will experience forceful contractions, and your body will be stretched beyond what you think possible. But when that is over, the pain will be forgotten, replaced with happiness. You have brought a child into the world.

Savour the moment of your baby's birth. Cherish your first embrace. Enjoy saying her name aloud. Tell her she is loved. Admire her features. Remember your husband's response. Enjoy the moment together. You have made this little person. And she is simply breathtaking.

Confession and prayer: Oh, the unspeakable joy of my baby's birth.

Week 39: Day 1

Psalm 71:6 (NLT) *I have relied on you from the day I was born. You brought me safely through birth, and I always praise you.*

Giving birth in a safe and healthy environment is something women of high income countries take for granted. The reality is that giving birth is dangerous. There are risks. More than modern medicine, birthing suites, and doulas, your baby's birth will be safe because the Word promises it. It is wonderful to have the added security of such things, but the most important reason you and baby will be safe is because God says so.

Science is often credited with improvements in childbirth and infant mortality. I personally believe that God's grace has brought about medical improvements in high income countries - nations that were established on God's Word. His wisdom and knowledge have caused greater safety during childbirth.

God has placed great doctors, midwives, and medical professionals in your pregnancy journey. They will draw on His wisdom to bring your baby securely into the world, whether they acknowledge this or not.

Confession and prayer: I believe that You, Lord, will bring my baby safely through birth.

Week 39: Day 2

Job 1:21 (NLT) *He said, "I came naked from my mother's womb and I will be naked when I leave. The Lord gave me what I had, and the Lord has taken it away. Praise the name of the Lord!"*

Everyone in life starts out the same. We all begin with nothing. It is amazing how quickly that changes. Within days your baby's cupboards will be full of clothes, her toy chest overflowing with toys, and her nursery bursting with things for her to enjoy. All these things are a blessing of the Lord.

Job had amassed great wealth, but he also had great humility. He knew that everything he had, from his first nappy, to his home and family, came from God.

I can almost guarantee that your child will be spoilt. If she knows it is not of her own effort, but because of the grace of God, she will maintain humility and graciousness.

Bless your child with beautiful things, but also bless her with the knowledge of God's goodness. Teach true humility. She has been brought into the world to use her gifts as a blessing to others.

Confession and prayer: I determine to show my baby that every good thing in her life is from You.

Week 39: Day 3

Isaiah 46:3 (NKJV) *"Listen to Me, O house of Jacob, and all the remnant of the house of Israel, who have been upheld by Me from birth, who have been carried from the womb."*

If you haven't picked up on this already, I love the imagery of Scripture. In the Word, Father paints such gorgeous pictures of His activity in our lives. Here in Isaiah 46, we see that He is at work in a beautiful way during a baby's delivery. He carries babies, from the safety of mother's womb, into the world. It is not a scary or foreign place when you are carried in the hands of God.

Talk to your baby about her birth. As you do, tell her that the world is a wonderful home. She need not be afraid about exiting her dwelling of nine months. The Lord, her magnificent Shepherd, will carry her through the womb, and into your arms. Nothing will go wrong. She will be protected and upheld by His strong arm.

If The Lord carries you through life, He will most certainly carry your baby into the world.

Confession and prayer: Thank You, Jesus, for carrying my baby from the womb.

Week 39: Day 4

Galatians 1:15 (MSG) *Why, when I was still in my mother's womb he chose and called me out of sheer generosity!*

When you are at the end of your pregnancy it can feel as though you have been pregnant forever. You may be thinking, "Will this baby ever come out?" Yes, she will. Her time of development inside your body is complete. Father God is now calling her out of the womb. He says, "Little one, it is time for you to go into the world. You don't have to be afraid. There are such awesome things to discover. Come out! Come out into the world."

As the next few days go by, keep confessing that God is calling your baby out. She might be comfortable in there, but the time has come for her to join your family on the outside. And if your due date comes and goes, don't despair. Every day is a day closer to meeting this new person. Things will happen sooner than you think. God is calling her out. Can you hear Him?

Confession and prayer: Father, thank You for calling my baby out of the womb.

Week 39: Day 5

Psalm 22:10 (CEV) *From the day I was born, I have been in your care, and from the time of my birth, you have been my God.*

I became a Christian when I was eight years old. Growing up, I looked down on my upbringing. I wished that I had a real testimony. One where I could say that God saved me from prison, drugs, gangs, or something like that. My life and Christian testimony seemed boring.

I don't see it that way now. I am thankful that I have lived virtually my entire life as a Christian. I am grateful that I never got involved in drugs, gangs, or crime. And has my life been boring? Hardly. It has been exciting and full of happiness, because I followed Jesus.

It is a tremendous privilege bringing a child into the world who will know Jesus from the outset. There is no more wonderful life than calling Him God as a young child. Impress on her that it is the greatest testimony when you can say, "From the time of my birth, You have been my God."

Confession and prayer: My heart's desire for my child is that she will say, "From the time of my birth, You have been my God."

Week 39: Day 6

Isaiah 66:9 (CEV) *The LORD is the one who makes birth possible. And he will see that Zion has many more children. The LORD has spoken.*

God's Word is full of promises for things we face in life today. You just have to look for them. Isaiah 66:9 states that it is God who makes birth possible. Nothing we do is independent of Him. As you give birth to your child, be mindful that God has brought it about. He makes it possible, and orchestrates the whole process. When He is in the birthing suite nothing will go wrong.

The second promise is great for those wanting a larger family: He will see that you can have more children. If this child is your last, and you have decided to shut up shop, be blessed. But if you want to have more children, God will see to it that you do. Don't be fearful or worried when you decide it is time to have another child. He who makes birth possible, is also in charge of conception in the future.

There are promises in the Bible about birth and having more children. Now that you know them, claim the promises as your own.

Confession and prayer: Father, I believe that You will enable me to have more children in the future.

Week 39: Day 7

Ecclesiastes 3:1-2a (MSG) *There's an opportune time to do things, a right time for everything on the earth: A right time for birth...*

The Lord is not a God of luck or chance. He is a God of right timing and happenings. God has ordained for things to happen at the best time. He has done that throughout your life. There was a right time for you to meet your husband, there was a right time for you to be in your current job. There are right timings for certain relationships and associations. Being in the right place at the right time is a part of his grace and favour on your life.

There is also a right time for your baby to be born. That time is now. Confess this to your body. Command your body to prepare itself for delivering your baby. Declare this to your baby. The womb is no longer a comfortable place for her. Your placenta will start to disintegrate as you pass your due date. Don't worry, that is all part of the process. Your baby needs different nutrition. It is time for her to be born. It is the opportune moment. Now is the right time for birth.

Confession and prayer: Baby, now is the time for you to be born!

Week 40: Day 1

Psalm 22:9 (CEV) *You, LORD, brought me safely through birth, and you protected me when I was a baby at my mother's breast.*

Psalm 22:9 provides a wonderful promise to new parents. A promise of protection while their child is young. Young children are vulnerable to sickness, but the Lord promises protection in that susceptible time. As He will bring your baby safety through birth, He will provide protection when she is an infant.

If any diseases threaten your child during the early months of her life, remember to proclaim this verse. The Blood of Jesus provides protection for your baby. God's will is not for her to suffer.

Breast feeding provides immunity to a child through her mother's milk. However, if you have chosen not to breast feed, God will protect your baby, and give her the immunity she needs. Don't feel guilty. His immunity and protection is greater. And if you are able to breastfeed, your baby's immunity and protection are from the Lord too. It is a powerful promise.

Confession and prayer: Father, I thank You for the Blood of Jesus, providing protection for my baby while she is small.

Week 40: Day 2

Luke 1:14 (CEV) *His birth will make you very happy, and many people will be Glad.*

Babies bring such joy and gladness into the world. Your child will be no exception. Enjoy her first few days. Cherish the love and gifts others shower upon her. The first days of your baby's life are heavenly days.

Don't allow anything to steal your joy. Things such as the way in which your child was born, struggles with breastfeeding, or sleep deprivation, can try to rob you of the happiness of baby entering the world. You will never be able to relive the wonder of the first days of baby's life. Be happy. Let nothing stress or bother you. Be immune to how others feel. May her birth make you blissfully happy. Overjoyed.

Choose to remember the happy joyous time surrounding your child's birth. Believe the best, stay positive, but most importantly, don't hide your happiness. Your baby has been born. It is time to rejoice.

Confession and prayer: I will happily enjoy the first days of my baby's life. Nothing will rob my joy.

Week 40: Day 3

1 Peter 2:9 (NLT) *But you are not like that, for you are a chosen people. You are royal priests, a holy nation, God's very own possession. As a result, you can show others the goodness of God, for he called you out of the darkness into his wonderful light.*

When my child visited the doctor recently, he asked to look inside my son's mouth. "It's dark inside your body, that's why I use this little light," the doctor said as he shone a small torch into his mouth.

It is dark inside our bodies. Of course it is. But this fact is possibly something that you have never thought about. Not that you should. I bring this to your attention because right now, your baby, is in darkness. She has been living in darkness for the past nine months.

But she is a chosen one, God's very own possession. As a consequence, Father is calling her out of darkness into His wonderful light. Hold that thought. It is beautiful.

Pray this passage of Scripture over your baby all day. She is part of a royal priesthood, servants of the Most High. Today, God calls her out of the darkness of the womb into His marvellous light.

Confession and prayer: Lord, I can hear You calling my baby out of darkness into Your wondrous light.

Week 40: Day 4

Psalm 8:2 (MSG) *Nursing infants gurgle choruses about you; toddlers shout the songs that drown out enemy talk, and silence atheist babble.*

Babies make the cutest sounds. Gentle coos, sweet babbles, blowing bubbles. Of course, they can also wail loudly, but we won't get into that.

Have you wondered what it is babies are trying to say? They make gorgeous sounds, with concerned looks, that indicate they are trying to say something. But what? Psalm 8:2 sheds some insight: babies are singing songs to the Lord that drown out the devil and silence atheists! How cool is that?

When your child looks at you, and babbles in her sweet, angelic way, know that she is doing more than whispering sweet nothings. She is drowning out the lies of the devil that come against your marriage and family, with a song from Heaven. And her song is so profound that it silences atheists. Perhaps you know people who don't believe there is a God. Make sure they get a nurse. Her song will change their heart.

Confession and prayer: Thank You, Jesus for the beautiful sounds my child will make, sounds of praise to You.

Week 40: Day 5

Psalm 119:97 (MSG) *Oh, how I love all you've revealed; I reverently ponder it all the day long.*

Your child's birth is precious. Regardless of how she is revealed, if you hold a healthy child in your arms, you are blessed. The days and months that follow are also precious moments, things to ponder.

You may have the type of personality that records everything, or you may barely take photos. If you can recite when she reached all her milestones, or even if you can't, cherish every moment. You have no doubt heard this before, but time goes fast. Nothing is more important than spending quality time with your baby, even if it is gazing at her while she sleeps.

The washing can wait, the dishes will get done eventually, make the time to enjoy moments when they happen. Stuff comes up. Let baby be your priority. Make memories that you can look back on with fondness. Moments that you can ponder, all day long.

Confession and prayer: Making precious memories with my baby will always be my priority.

Week 40: Day 6

Psalm 31:14 (NKJV) *But as for me, I trust in You, O Lord; I say, "You are my God."*

Due date about to arrive, bag packed, nursery ready, all you need now is the baby! You have been praying and believing for peace, strength, and courage for the past nine months. Time is almost up. Whatever happens, may you echo the sentiment of the psalmist, "As for me, I trust the Lord, He is my God."

All the work is done. The only thing you have to do now is trust. God will come good on His promises. He is faithful. He is trustworthy. Your baby will be born. She will be healthy. You will experience a fabulous labour and delivery. Recovery will be quick and without complications.

And if things go wrong?
"I trust in You, O Lord. You are my God."

He is always God. He is always good. Trust Him. Love Him. His grace is sufficient for you, and every situation.

"Yes, Lord, You are my God."

Confession and prayer: Whatever life brings, O Lord, You are my God. I ever trust in You.

Week 40: Day 7

Psalm 118:24 (NLT) *This is the day the Lord has made. We will rejoice and be glad in it.*

Today is a marvellous day. Your due date is tomorrow. You can rejoice and be glad in this day. The Lord has made it. It is a good day.

If tomorrow comes and goes, and the next day, and the next, and baby still has not arrived, don't be discouraged. Rejoice and be glad in each day. You are one step closer to seeing your child face to face.

So whether baby arrives on time or is, er, fashionably late, rejoice. Be glad! There is not long now. You are healthy and strong. The Lord is with you. His protection, grace, and favour are upon you. He has placed you in a wonderful family, with supportive friends to assist you in this new stage. You have much to be grateful for. You are blessed with every spiritual blessing, crowned with love and compassion. Yes, today is a day to rejoice.

Confession and prayer: Lord, I will rejoice and be glad in this day that You have made.

This is how God feels about you

It is overwhelming to know that the God of Heaven cares about you. His love for you is immense.

How do you respond to such grandiose love? Give Him your life. Believe in Jesus. Believe that He died on the Cross in your place.

Follow these steps:

Admit to God you've messed up, regardless of how "good" you think you've been compared to others.
Believe that Jesus died for your mistakes and ask for forgiveness.
Follow God's destiny for your life.

You can pray a prayer like this: *Jesus, I am sorry for all the things I have ever done, that have brought hurt upon myself, others and especially You. I believe that You paid the price for my sin on the Cross. I believe You have an awesome plan for my life and I intend to follow it as long as I live. Come into my life and make me the person You destined me to become. Thank you for saving me. In Your name, Amen.*

If you welcomed Jesus into your life angels are rejoicing over your decision! Take time to pray and read the Bible everyday and allow God's promises to become real in your life.

This is just the beginning of the big plans God has for you!

Before you go...

If Expecting Daily Pregnancy Devotion has blessed you during pregnancy, please write a review.

Also, don't forget to access the Freebies that are a companion to the devotional.
Access them here: sarahcoleman.com.au/expecting-freebies/

Here's a few other titles by Sarah Coleman:

Single Christian Female

Make Yourself Amazing

Unveiled

Be amazing

Together: A Journey of Godly Marriage

CPSIA information can be obtained
at www.ICGtesting.com
Printed in the USA
BVOW06s1233250717

490155BV00011B/68/P

9 781366 892416